Simple and Practical

Book-Keeping

How to Create a
Complete and Accurate
Book-keeping System

Keith Kirkland and Stuart Howard

**KOGAN
PAGE**

<u>YOURS TO HAVE AND TO HOLD</u>
BUT NOT TO COPY

First published in 1998

Kogan Page Limited
120 Pentonville Road
London N1 9JN

© Vector Business Development, 1998

Illustrations by John Loader

British Library Cataloguing in Publication Data

A CIP record for this book is available from the British Library

ISBN 0 7494 2927 5

Typeset by Vector Business Development.
Printed and bound in Great Britain by Bell & Bain Ltd, Glasgow.

Contents

Chapter 1

Introduction

Why Keep Books?

Let's be honest, book-keeping can be a bit of a chore at times! However, it is an essential business skill. In essence, book-keeping is very simple. The book-keeper collects information about the business and *organises* it. Once organised, the records can be used to:

- check that all income and expenditure has been properly accounted for
- provide information which helps manage the business efficiently.

Here are five good reasons for keeping books.

Financial Control

Good financial control is essential for the survival of any business. Businesses which keep proper records are able to determine their financial standing at any time. At the very least, you want to know:

- how much money have I got now?
- where does my money come from?
- where does my money go to?
- how much do I owe others?
- how much do other people owe me?
- am I trading profitably?

If you produce a cashflow forecast and check your progress using your book-keeping records, you will have a very good idea of your financial standing at any time.

Some people put all their paper work into a shoe box and wait until the accountant comes round to sort it out. This makes no sense because:

- they won't have information about the business when they need it
- they won't be able to control their credit transactions
- their accountant's bills will be sky high
- they will get behind with their VAT returns and probably attract a fine
- they may have trouble complying with the rules of 'self assessment' (which could also attract a fine).

Lack of financial information is a major reason for business failure.

Taxation

The government uses business to collect many taxes. Although the business is not paid for collecting taxes, it can suffer severe penalties for failing to collect the right amounts of tax. Most businesses are involved in the collection of:

- PAYE
- VAT
- National Insurance
- Schedule D or Corporation Tax.

Good records are needed for tax administration.

Accountancy Fees

Most businesses use an accountant to calculate their profit and agree the tax liability with the Inland Revenue. If you have good records, the accountant will be able to produce accounts quickly and economically. If your records are a mess, the accountant will have to spend time collecting basic data together. Because accountants' fees are based on time spent, you will pay higher fees if your records are poor.

Bank Borrowing

At some point in time, most businesses need to borrow money from the bank. Banks like to see past accounts as a guide to business profitability. Banks also like to see some form of business controls in place. This gives them confidence that the debt will be repaid as agreed.
An accurate, complete and up-to-date book-keeping system will supply the information needed to convince the bank that you know what you are doing.

Self Assessment

A new method of taxation was introduced from the tax year 1996/97 called self assessment. Self assessment is a system of taxation which will affect:

- most employees who receive expenses and benefits
- all sole traders and business partners.

Every individual affected by self assessment needs to complete a tax return and calculate his or her tax liability.

Under self assessment, there are strict rules governing both the quality of business records and the period over which these records must be retained. The Inland Revenue will expect a business to keep the following records for at least five years after submission of the self assessment form.

- A record of all sales and other business receipts, together with supporting documents (eg invoices, bank statements, paying-in slips etc).

- A record of all normal business expenditure (eg wages, materials, rent, expenses and benefits etc).

- A record of all assets purchased and sold by the business. This would include items like machinery and vehicles etc.

- A record of all capital introduced into the business from personal funds.

Failure to upkeep and retain such records could lead to high penalties. If you keep your books in the way we recommend, you will be able to show your tax inspector that your record keeping is up to the mark!

The Analysed Cashbook

There are many ways of keeping books. This book explains how to keep records using a cashbook. This is a simple, flexible book-keeping system which suits most businesses. The use of the word 'cashbook' is interesting. In the old days, all transactions were in cash so the book was called a cashbook. Nowadays money changes hands in many different ways, eg by cheque, direct debit, credit card etc. Perhaps we should now call it a 'money book' rather than a 'cashbook'. *All* money transactions are included in the 'cashbook'. However, old habits die hard so we will probably still be talking about 'cashbooks' in the third millennium!

Keeping the books

The analysed cashbook can take several forms:

- you can use loose leaves which are held in place in a ring binder, or
- you can use a bound analysis book
- if you have access to a personal computer, you can use a computerised version of the cashbook. This can save a lot of time and effort.

We will begin by having a look at the manual cashbook. If you are new to book-keeping, we suggest you start with loose leaves of paper. You may need several attempts before you hit on the format which suits your business. Loose leaves are much cheaper to experiment with.

An example of analysis paper is shown on page 7 (which is printed sideways). Columns on the left hand side are used to record 'income'; columns on the right hand side are used to record 'expenditure'. Worked examples are shown on later pages of this book (eg pages 33, 57 and 116).

Because there always seem to be more ways of spending money than acquiring it, the page is not divided into two equal halves! The left hand side (for income) tends to be narrower, often having around eight columns. The right hand side (for payments) tends to be wider, often having around sixteen columns.

Most people prefer to use a *bound* cashbook. This is simply a collection of loose leaves permanently bound together. You will find many different layouts available at the stationers. They are labelled according to the number of columns allocated to each side of the cashbook. For example, if you see one labelled 7/10, this means that there are seven columns for income (ie the left side) and ten columns for expenditure (ie the right side). Cashbooks are available in many versions, one of which will almost certainly fit your business. We will look at different ways to use cashbooks in Chapters 3, 4 and 6.

Before we do this, however, we need to look at Value Added Tax (VAT) because it plays a big part when deciding the format in which you keep your books. Your book-keeping layout will vary according to whether you are:

- not VAT registered
- VAT registered – accounting for VAT on the 'cash accounting' scheme
- VAT registered – accounting for VAT according to the 'tax point date' on the invoice.

If you're unsure about VAT then you may find the notes in Chapter 2 useful. These VAT notes will enable you to check which book-keeping method suits any particular business as follows:

Not VAT registered   –   Chapter 3

On the 'Cash Accounting' scheme –   Chapter 4

On 'Tax Point Accounting'   –   Chapter 6

If you are reading these notes with only one particular business in mind, it may be tempting to read only the chapter relating to 'your' business. However, we suggest that you look at each chapter because we have not duplicated every piece of information in every chapter. For example, credit control is not introduced until Chapter 6; however, even small businesses which offer credit will need some form of credit control.

Be sure to read Chapters 7 and 8. These cover:

Filing your Records   –   Chapter 7

Petty Cash   –   Chapter 8

These chapters should prove useful whichever book-keeping system you use.

An Example of Analysis Paper

Income		Expenditure

Income is recorded on this side

Expenditure is recorded on this side

Chapter 2

Introduction to Value Added Tax

It may seem strange looking at value added tax before considering book-keeping methods. However, VAT has a profound effect on the way you keep your books. We have suggested that you use different methods of book-keeping according to whether you are:

- not registered for VAT
- on the cash accounting scheme
- accounting for VAT based on the tax point date.

If you are new to value added tax, we hope you will find the following notes useful. At the end of this section, you will know which book-keeping system fits your current VAT registration status.

What is VAT?

VAT can be described as:

> *'A tax on final consumer spending, collected in stages, when goods change hands or services are performed'.*

Almost any commercial transaction can be liable to VAT. Transactions which are liable for VAT are called 'taxable supplies'.

Examples include:

- the sale of goods
- the performance of a service
- an exchange of goods or services, *or*
- a gift in kind.

The administration, collection and enforcement of VAT is the responsibility of HM Customs and Excise. Each registered trader will have a local VAT office which administers the scheme locally. This is the trader's local contact point. All queries should be conducted through your local VAT office. The VAT Central Unit at Southend-on-Sea maintains a central record of registered persons. Southend is responsible for the issue of VAT returns. It also processes VAT collections and reimbursements.

Categories and Rates of VAT

There are three categories of VAT. These are standard rate, zero rate and exempt supplies. The following table gives some examples.

Category	Example	Rate
Exempt	Insurance Postal services Finance Education Health and welfare Betting, gaming and lotteries Burial and cremation	No tax applies
		Continued

Category	Example	Rate
Zero Rate	Most food	Nil %
	Children's clothes	
	Educational books	
	Water and sewage services	
	Drugs/medicines on prescription	
Standard Rate	Stationery	17½%
	Accountants' fees	
	Petrol and diesel	
	(In effect, any goods or	
	services which are not in	
	the previous categories)	

(VAT is rated at 5% on domestic fuel and power. Fuel and power supplied commercially is standard rated.)

The above list is by no means definitive. There are exceptions for most of the examples.

If you are not sure whether your supplies are standard rated, zero rated or exempt, talk to your local VAT office or accountant. Alternatively, read the General VAT Guide (Notice No: 700) which should offer sufficient guidance to answer your queries. It is obtainable from your local VAT office which is listed under Customs and Excise in your telephone directory.

Of course, VAT doesn't apply to everything. Some items are outside the scope of VAT. Examples include:

- wages, salaries, drawings
- loan repayments
- road tax
- rates.

11

The Difference between Zero Rated and Exempt Supplies

Many people are unsure of the difference between zero rated and exempt supplies. Let's see if we can make this clear.

Zero Rated Supplies

At first sight, zero rate VAT may seem rather pointless because no tax is collected. However, zero rated VAT has one very important aspect. Zero rated supplies count towards your taxable (or 'VATable') turnover. Your taxable turnover determines whether you have to register for VAT or not.

In fact, if all of your sales are zero rated, you can be in a very favoured position. You can reclaim all the VAT charged by your suppliers without the need to collect VAT from your customers!

Exempt Supplies

Exempt supplies are quite different. Exempt supplies do not count towards taxable turnover. If all your supplies to customers are exempt, you will never need to register for VAT (because you cannot exceed the registration limit). Since you cannot be VAT registered, you cannot of course charge your customers VAT. Nor will you be able to recover value added tax charged to you by your suppliers.

Partial Exemption

The situation regarding businesses that make both exempt and chargeable supplies is slightly more complex. This is called partial exemption. Take advice before setting up your book-keeping system from either the VAT office or your accountant.

Registration

A business has to register for VAT if the total value of taxable supplies in the past twelve months exceeds the VAT registration limit. This is known as mandatory registration. The registration limit is usually revised each year. For example, it was set at £50,000 with effect from 1 April 1998. Remember only *taxable* turnover counts towards the registration limit. If you only deal in exempt supplies then none of your turnover counts towards the taxable limit. On the other hand, don't forget to include zero rated supplies (ie sales VATable at zero per cent) since these *do* count towards the registration limit.

By the way, you are also required to register for VAT if you *believe* that the value of taxable supplies in the next 30 days will exceed the annual limit.

Normally you have no choice whether to register for VAT once you have exceeded the registration limit. However, there is one exception. If you find that your taxable turnover has exceeded the limit for the past year but you believe that it will not exceed this level in the next twelve months, then you probably don't need to register. This would apply if the past year's turnover was an exceptional 'blip' and unlikely to be repeated again. Check your position with the VAT office for peace of mind.

Registration is a simple process which only requires you to complete VAT Form 1. Once registered, you will be given a VAT number and a date from which you must charge your customers value added tax.

Voluntary Registration

If your business turnover has not reached the mandatory registration limit, you can still register for VAT voluntarily. This enables traders to reclaim VAT on purchases. However, they must then charge VAT on sales.

This will benefit traders whose *customers* are registered for VAT. Since customers can reclaim VAT charged to them, they don't mind whether your bills to them include VAT or not. However, as a registered trader, you will be able to reclaim value added tax on all your purchases which have VAT levied on them.

If your customers are not VAT registered (eg private persons), you probably won't want to register voluntarily. This is because you will have to charge them VAT which may erode the price advantage that you could enjoy over a VAT registered trader.

Deregistration

If you are currently VAT registered, you can deregister provided you believe that your taxable turnover in the next twelve months will fall below the deregistration limit. For example this limit was set at £48,000 from 1 April 1998. There are often hidden costs in deregistration. For example, you must charge yourself VAT on the market value of any items retained within the business on which VAT has been reclaimed. It is best, therefore, to take advice prior to deregistration.

How does VAT Work?

There are two sides to VAT:

Output tax   This is the tax charged by you on supplies of goods or services to your customers.

Input tax   This is the tax charged to you on items purchased from your suppliers.

Normally traders collect more tax from their customers than they pay their suppliers. They pay the surplus to Customs and Excise. Most businesses account for VAT quarterly. At the end of each quarter, they complete their quarterly return and remit the surplus VAT, with the VAT return, to Customs and Excise. This can be represented diagrammatically as follows:

Output tax	*minus*	**Input tax**	*equals*	**VAT payable**

However, not all traders collect more than they pay out. A few traders pay out more VAT than they collect. These traders are entitled to a refund from Customs and Excise. For example, traders who only sell zero rated goods will almost always get a VAT refund as their output tax is charged at a nil rate of tax.

From what has been said so far, you will realise that a business is neither richer nor poorer as a result of collecting value added tax. If the trader collects a VAT surplus, he pays it to Customs and Excise. If he pays out more VAT than he collects, he reclaims the difference from HMC&E. The net effect for the registered trader is, therefore, nil. Unfortunately, the trader has to expend a great deal of time and effort to produce this nil result. Value added tax is normally borne by the final (ie VAT unregistered) customer.

The diagram on page 16 will help to make this clear. It shows the chain of transactions relating to an imaginary furniture maker. The diagram traces the transactions from the timber grower to the final customer. Note how each trader pays the surplus to HMC&E. Only the final customer suffers the tax (which is £35 in this case).

VAT Example

Trader Costs			Sale Price excl VAT	VAT	Sale Price incl 17½% VAT	VAT Paid to HMC&E	
Supplier							
						Output tax	£5.25
	Labour	£25					
			£30	£5.25	£35.25	Input tax	Nil
	Profit	£5					
						VAT due to HMC&E	£5.25
Manufacturer							
	Material	£30				Output tax	£21.00
	Labour	£65	£120	£21.00	£141.00	Input tax	£5.25
	Profit	£25				VAT due to HMC&E	£15.75
Wholesaler							
	Material	£120				Output tax	£26.25
	Other	£10	£150	£26.25	£176.25	Input tax	£21.00
	Profit	£20				VAT due to HMC&E	£5.25
Retailer							
	Goods	£150				Output tax	£35.00
	Other	£30	£200	£35.00	£235.00	Input tax	£26.25
	Profit	£20				VAT due to HMC&E	£8.75

Total Tax Paid by Customer £35.00

The VAT Fraction

Most of the invoices that you receive will clearly show the amount of VAT charged to you. However, small receipts (like parking, retail sales, petrol etc) may not identify the VAT separately. You must be able to extract VAT from bills which don't have the VAT separately identified.

Some people believe that since VAT is calculated by *adding* 17½% to the purchase price then VAT must be extracted by *subtracting* 17½% from the VAT inclusive price.

This is not correct. If you do this, you will pay the wrong amount of VAT.

The general formula for extracting VAT is as follows:

$$\text{Amount of VAT} = \frac{\text{Rate of VAT}}{100 + \text{rate of VAT}}$$

If value added tax is 17½% then:

$$\text{Amount of VAT} = \frac{17\frac{1}{2}}{100 + 17\frac{1}{2}} = \frac{17\frac{1}{2}}{117\frac{1}{2}} \text{ which equates to } \frac{7}{47}$$

This means that to calculate the amount of VAT in a VAT inclusive price, you must multiply the VAT inclusive price by 7/47.

Here is an example. Suppose that we have a bill for £235 including VAT. The VAT element of this bill must be:

$$\frac{7}{47} \times 235 = £35$$

Therefore, the net price would have been £235 – £35 = £200

Now have a go at working out the VAT on the following four amounts. Check your answer with page 157.

> **Exercise 1**
>
> Work out the VAT included in the following VAT inclusive prices:
>
> £150
>
> £290
>
> £56
>
> £2,670

The Annual Accounting Scheme

Normally a trader will complete the VAT return based on the previous quarter's trading. Small firms, however, can elect to 'settle' their VAT account annually. There are two provisos:

- they must have been registered for 12 months, *and*
- they must have a taxable turnover below the annual accounting limit (at the time of writing these notes, this limit was £300,000).

The trader is required to make nine equal 'standing orders' which are designed to clear the estimated liability. A final adjustment is made at the end of the year.

The Cash Accounting Scheme

This scheme applies to registered businesses with an annual turnover below the cash accounting limit. This limit was £437,500 at the time of writing these notes. These traders can account for VAT based on the date when *payments* are received and made, instead of using the *tax invoice* dates. Firms using the cash accounting scheme could show significant cash flow benefits as well as simplified paperwork. Don't worry if this isn't clear, cash accounting is explained in more detail in Chapter 4.

The VAT Quarterly Return

Once you are VAT registered, you will have to complete a quarterly return (this is done using VAT Form 100). An example of this is shown on pages 21 and 22. This is issued by the Central Unit at Southend. It should be completed within a month of the end of the VAT quarter to which it relates and returned to Southend together with any payment which may be due. Failure to make the return, pay the VAT or to make false statements or submit a late return can attract a fine from HM Customs and Excise.

The main items of information required on the VAT return are:

- output tax charged to customers, ie the VAT collected on your sales (box 1)
- input tax charged by suppliers, ie the VAT paid on your purchases (box 4)
- net VAT to be paid to (or reclaimed from) Customs and Excise (box 5)
- total value of sales excluding VAT for the quarter (box 6)
- total value of purchases excluding VAT for the quarter (box 7)
- sales and purchase information relating to transactions with other members of the EEC (boxes 2, 8 and 9).

Most traders submit a VAT quarterly return; however, you have the option to submit returns monthly. The extra effort involved in reclaiming monthly will only be attractive to traders claiming substantial refunds of value added tax.

Most traders calculate their VAT by analysing VAT inputs and VAT outputs. Do be aware, however, that there are special schemes which apply to retailers. This is because many retailers sell a variety of goods that fall into different VAT categories, eg standard rated, zero rated etc. Special schemes provide for an easier way of calculating VAT instead of analysing each sale. If you are a retailer, check the VAT guide to see if any of these schemes are attractive to you.

VAT Charges on Vehicles

VAT on Vehicle Purchase

In general, you can reclaim VAT on vans and goods vehicles. Normally, you cannot reclaim VAT on passenger cars. If a car is used *wholly* for business (ie no private use), it may be possible to recover the VAT; however this will only apply in very exceptional circumstances. Check the VAT guide Notice 700 for the fine print.

VAT on Fuel

In general, VAT on fuel purchased for business use is reclaimable. However, many vehicles used for business are also used privately. VAT is not reclaimable on the private use of a business vehicle. It is very difficult, however, to differentiate between business and private mileage unless a detailed log is  kept. To overcome this, HMC&E have set an annual scale charge which is used to account for fuel used privately. The scale charge is deemed to cover all your private mileage, irrespective of how high or low it actually is. In practice, there are two scale charges depending on whether the vehicle uses petrol or diesel fuel. For example, the scale charges per quarter from 6 April 1998 were set at:

Cylinder Capacity		Scale Charge*	VAT due per car
Diesel Engine	2000cc or less	£196	£29.19
	More than 2000cc	£248	£36.93
Petrol Engine	1400cc or less	£212	£31.57
	Over 1400cc up to 2000cc	£268	£39.91
	Over 2000cc	£396	£58.97

* Scale charge includes VAT

Value Added Tax Return

For the period

HM Customs and Excise

For Official Use

Registration Number

Period

You could be liable to a financial penalty it your completed return and all the VAT payable are not received by the due date.

Due date:

For Official Use

Your VAT Office telephone number is

Before you fill in this form please read the notes on the back and the VAT leaflet *"Filling in your VAT return".* Fill in all boxes clearly in ink, and write 'none' where necessary. Don't put a dash or leave any box blank. If there are no pence write "**00**" in the pence column. **Do not** enter more than one amount in any box.

For official use		£	p
VAT due in this period on **sales** and other outputs	1		
VAT due in this period on **acquisitions** from other **EC Member States**	2		
Total VAT due **(the sum of boxes 1 and 2)**	3		
VAT reclaimed in this period on **purchases** and other inputs (including acquisitions from the EC)	4		
Net VAT to be paid to Customs or reclaimed by you **(Difference between boxes 3 and 4)**	5		
Total value of **sales** and all other outputs excluding any VAT. **Include your box 8 figure**	6		00
Total value of **purchases** and all other inputs excluding any VAT. **Include your box 9 figure**	7		00
Total value of all **supplies** of goods and related services, excluding any VAT, to other **EC Member States**	8		00
Total value of all **acquisitions** of goods and related services, excluding any VAT, from other **EC Member States**	9		00

Retail schemes. If you have used any of the schemes in the period covered by this return, enter the relevant letter(s) in this box.

If you are enclosing a payment please tick this box.

DECLARATION: You, or someone on your behalf, must sign below.

I,...declare that the
(Full name of signatory in BLOCK LETTERS)

information given above is true and complete.

Signature...Date.............19......

A false declaration can result in prosecution.

L

VAT 100

Notes

These notes and the VAT leaflet *Filling in your VAT Return* will help you fill in this form. You may also need to refer to other VAT notices and leaflets.

If you need help or advice please contact your local VAT office.

If you are using the 'cash accounting scheme', the amounts of VAT due and deductible are for payments you actually receive and make, and not on invoices you receive and send out.

If you put **minus figures** in boxes 1 to 3 or are entering a sum **DUE** to Customs in box 4, please enclose the figure in brackets.

Amounts not declared correctly on previous returns

1. If any of your previous returns declared too much or too little VAT that has not yet been accounted for, you can correct the position using boxes 1 and 4 for net amounts of **£2000 or less.**

2. If the net amount is **over £2000**, tell your local VAT office immediately. Don't include the amount on this return.

If you do not follow these instructions you could be liable to a financial penalty.

How to pay your VAT

Cross all cheques and postal orders "AC Payee Only" make them payable to "H M Customs and Excise" and put a line through any spaces on the "pay" line.

In your own interest do not send notes, coins, or uncrossed postal orders by post.

If you wish to pay by 'credit transfer', ask your local VAT office. Pre-printed booklets of credit transfer slips will be sent to you.

Please write your VAT registration number on the back of all cheques and bank giro credit slips.

Where to send this return

You must make sure your completed form and any VAT payable are received by the 'due date' (shown over the page) by:
The Controller
VAT Central Unit
H M Customs and Excise
21 Victoria Avenue
Southend-on-Sea X
SS99 1AA.

Complaints

The Adjudicator reviews complaints not settled to your satisfaction by Customs. The recommendations of the Adjudicator are independent and the service is free. It covers complaints not general enquiries. [Telephone the Adjudicator on 0171 930 2292].

VAT 100

Box 1

Show the VAT due on all goods and services you supplied in this period.

Box 2

Show the VAT due (but not paid) on all goods and related services you acquired in this period from other EC Member States.

Box 3

Show the total amount of the VAT due ie the sum of boxes 1 and 2. This is your total **Output** tax.

Box 4

Show the amount of VAT deductible on any business purchases including acquisitions of goods and related services from other EC Member States. This is your **Input** tax.

Box 5

If this amount is under £1, you need not send any payment, nor will any repayment be made to you, but you must still fill in this form and send it to the VAT Central Unit.

Boxes 6 and 7

In box 6 show the value excluding VAT of your total outputs (supplies of goods and services). Include zero rated, exempt outputs and EC supplies from box 8.

In box 7 show the value excluding VAT of all your inputs (purchases of goods and services). Include zero rated, exempt inputs and EC acquisitions from box 9.

Boxes 8 and 9

EC TRADE ONLY
Use these boxes if you have supplied goods to or acquired goods from another EC Member State. Include related services such as transport costs where these form part of the invoice or contract price. The figures should exclude VAT.

The other EC Member States are: Belgium, Denmark, France, Germany, Greece, Netherlands, Ireland, Italy, Luxembourg, Portugal, Spain, Austria, Finland and Sweden.

You must tell your local VAT office about any changes in your business circumstances (including changes of address).

When you fill in the VAT return, you need to make vehicle related entries in boxes 1 and 6. Add the VAT due for each car to the output tax figure in box 1. Add the gross scale charge *less* the VAT due to box 6 of the VAT return.

For example, if you had a petrol car of 1400cc or less, the VAT output tax to be added to box 1 would be £31.57. The amount to be recorded in box 6 would be the total scale charge of £212 less the VAT charge of £31.57. This is £180 when rounded up to the nearest whole pound.

Scale charges are generally adjusted annually in the budget. They relate to the tax year which runs from 6 April in one year to 5 April in the following year. Often a trader's VAT quarter will span the end of a tax year, eg a quarter may run over months March, April and May. In these circumstances, the new VAT charge is not applied until the first clear quarter arising in the new tax year. This means that there is no need to apportion scale charges.

VAT Records

- A taxable person must keep a record of all transactions and related documents for six years.
- A taxable person must keep records and accounts up to date.

VAT Inspections

All businesses are subject to routine control visits by HM Customs and Excise. Most new businesses receive a control visit shortly after registering. These visits are to check that the business is operating VAT correctly and to deal with any problems or questions that may arise. Customs and Excise have the right to check your records at any time.

VAT Penalties

Penalties can be imposed for:

- late registration
- serious misdeclaration
- persistent misdeclaration
- tax evasion
- failure to keep or produce VAT records
- unauthorised issue of tax invoices
- breaches of most of the other requirements under VAT law.

HM Customs and Excise can also charge 'default interest' on under-declarations and over-claims of VAT. Penalties can be severe.

Prompt and correctly completed returns and payments are the best way of avoiding trouble. In the event of problems, enter into early discussions with your local VAT office.

Trading with the European Community

From 1 January 1993 there was a change in the rules governing VAT accounting for businesses which export or import goods from another European Community state. Take advice from your accountant or the VAT office if you expect to export or import goods from these countries.

Trading with the European Community

Useful Information

All of the foregoing information can be found in the following Notices:

The VAT General Guide	–	Notice No: 700
Should I be Registered for VAT?	–	Notice No: 700/1/Dec95
The Ins and Outs of VAT	–	Notice No: 700/15/Mar95
Filling in your VAT Return	–	Notice No: 700/12/Sept95
Keeping Records and Accounts	–	Notice No: 700/21/Mar95

Requests for Notices and all queries regarding VAT should be made to your local VAT office. The address and telephone number is listed under 'Customs and Excise, Value Added Tax'.

How Should I Proceed?

The next three chapters explain how to keep books depending on your VAT registration status. These chapters are:

Book-keeping for non VAT registered traders – Chapter 3
Book-keeping for traders on cash accounting – Chapter 4
Book-keeping for traders on tax point accounting – Chapter 6

You may find it beneficial to read through all three chapters in sequence (even if you are only currently interested in one chapter). This is because:

– working through the chapters one after the other shows how book-keeping develops as VAT adds complications to the process.

– we develop new aspects like handling petty cash, day books, completing the VAT return one stage at a time as we proceed through the chapters.

Chapter 3

Book-keeping for Businesses which are not VAT Registered

This chapter applies if:

- your taxable turnover is below the annual registration limit, *and*
- you have not registered for VAT voluntarily.

If you have elected to register voluntarily, turn to Chapter 4.

Book-keeping for non-registered traders is very straight-forward. For example:

- you don't charge your customers VAT
- you don't suffer a VAT audit
- you don't make VAT returns
- you don't account for VAT on each item of income and expenditure (as you do if you are VAT registered).

As you are not VAT registered, you simply enter all expenditure *inclusive of VAT* in your cashbook. You obviously don't have VAT to account for on your sales because you will not be charging your customers VAT.

This saves you a lot of tedious work extracting VAT from your accounts. You will need to enter all income and expenditure in your cashbook alongside the date when you actually receive or pay the money. We will show you how to do this later in this section.

At the end of the year, your accountant will prepare your annual accounts on a VAT inclusive basis. Surprisingly, this means that you receive a small measure of tax relief on VAT you have paid on purchases. However, this is limited to the extent that VAT payments reduce your profits and, hence, the amount of income tax that you ultimately pay.

The best way to explain how book-keeping works for non-registered traders is by way of example. Let's see how it works for David and Jean's partnership.

David and Jean Example

David and Jean have been in partnership for some months. They buy old furniture which they renovate and sell from their small rented workshop. They are not registered for VAT.

They are using an analysed cashbook to record their business transactions. All income is entered on the left hand side of the cashbook. All expenditure is entered on the right hand side. Let's see how their cashbook is built up. If you want a sneak preview of the finished result, turn to page 33 now.

David

Jean

Recording Income

We started the month with £50 cash in hand brought forward from November. We received the following receipts in December.

Date	Transaction	Amount	Comments
		£	
Dec 1	Sale of 4 chairs	75.00	Cheque banked 1 Dec
8	Sale of table	40.00	Cash – NOT banked
14	Sale of old motor car	100.00	Cheque banked 14 Dec
16	Sale of bureau	97.50	Cheque banked 16 Dec
18	Sale of picture frame	125.00	Cheque banked 18 Dec
23	Insurance refund	20.00	Cheque banked 23 Dec

Notice that we have recorded these entries on the left hand side of the cashbook on page 33. The £50 cash brought forward has been entered on the first line of the income side in column 3. We have then missed a line to separate the brought forward figure from December's receipts. Notice that income is recorded in column 3 or column 4 according to whether the income arrives by cash or by cheque. We have labelled column 4 'cheques'; however, we would also include credit cards, BACS receipts, standing orders or direct debits into the business. All of these have to be processed through the bank account.

The income shown in columns 3 and 4 can be split into *type* of income. In our example, we have split income into 'sales income' in column 5 and 'other income' in column 6. It is very important to be able to identify 'sales' since you (and your accountant) will need the sales figure to construct your profit and loss account. 'Other' income must be clearly identified at this stage. 'Other' income receives different accounting treatment from sales income.

If David and Jean had been really keen, they could have split sales even further. For example, they could have had columns for sales of kitchen furniture, sales of bedroom furniture, sales of lounge furniture etc. This way they would be able to see at a glance which items were in most demand.

Once headings have been established, do not switch them around during the accounting year as this will confuse your accountant.

Handy Tip

It is important that you are consistent with your monthly headings. In fact, some book-keepers cut off the top part of the page (the bit which contains the column description). They then write the column descriptions on the cover page of the book. That way they avoid having to copy the headings onto every page of their cashbook.

We have already seen that income can arise in a variety of ways. Remember it is important that you enter *all* income including non-sales income. This will help your accountant to prepare your annual accounts.

Recording Expenditure

There are more columns on the expenditure side of the cashbook than the income side because greater analysis is required. Let's see how the following expenditures would be entered in the cashbook.

Date	Transaction	Amount	Comments
		£	
Dec 1	Banking	75.00	Entered in columns 10 & 16
1	Petrol	10.00	Cash
8	Telephone	29.50	Cheque
12	J Smith – materials	62.75	Cheque
14	Postage stamps	6.25	Cash
14	Banking	100.00	Entered in columns 10 & 16
15	Stationery	3.40	Cash
15	Jones – materials	16.50	Cheque
16	Banking	97.50	Entered in columns 10 & 16
16	Bank charges	6.25	Direct Debit
18	Banking	125.00	Entered in columns 10 & 16
23	Owners' Drawings	100.00	Cheque
23	Banking	20.00	Entered in columns 10 & 16

Notice that we have put the bank balance brought forward at the top of column 16 on page 33. We have also entered the transactions shown above in columns 7 to 16.

You can check that all of the income received on the income side of the cashbook has been accounted for on the expenditure side of the cashbook as follows.

Money can leave the business premises in one of two ways:

– it can be spent as cash, or
– it can be deposited with the bank.

Amounts spent as cash are recorded in column 9. Amounts of money deposited in the bank are recorded in columns 10 and 16. 'Bankings' can include cash, cheques, credit card slips etc. It may seem strange to record bankings in the expenditure side of the cashbook since the money is not 'spent' in the normal way. However, we need to account for all money which is no longer in our possession. In this instance, we are recording money which has left the business albeit, in this case, it has only been deposited in the bank.

By the way, amounts paid out of the bank by cheque, standing order, directs debits etc are recorded in column 11.

Analysis Columns

Columns 9 and 11 explain how money was spent, ie spent by cash (column 9) or via the bank in the form of a cheque, direct debit, standing order etc (column 11). However, it can be revealing to add extra columns which indicate how the money was spent. Most businesses have key items of expenditure which they need to keep an eye on. Typically these might be wages, materials, building occupancy costs etc. It can be worthwhile adding a column devoted to each key item of expenditure. These are shown in the example in columns 12 to 15. Items which are not key items of expenditure are lumped together in a miscellaneous column (column 15) which summarises other forms of expenditure incurred by the business. You can have as many analysis columns as you choose. However, if you have too many columns, the cashbook becomes unwieldy. In practice, half a dozen analysis columns will normally cover around 80% of your business expenditure. The rest can be left in the miscellaneous column.

Checking your Entries

In the exercises in this workbook, you can look up the answer in the Appendix to see if you got your figures right. In real life, things are not so simple; you can make mistakes by transposing figures, copying down wrong numbers, missing out entries for cash or bank etc. You need some way in which you can be *sure* that you have accounted for all income and expenditure. If you make the following checks, you can be confident that you have entered all your figures correctly.

David and Jean

December 19xx

Income

1	2	3	4	5	6
Date	Detail	Cash In	Cheques In	Sales	Other
	Cash Balance B/F	50 00			
Dec 1	Sale of Chairs		75 00	75 00	
8	Sale of Table	40 00		40 00	
14	Sale of Motor Car		100 00		100 00
16	Sale of Bureax		97 50	97 50	
18	Sale of Picture Frame		125 00	125 00	
23	Insurance Refund		20 00		20 00
	Column Totals	40 00	417 50	337 50	120 00

457.50

457.50

Cross Casting this Month's Income
(Excluding brought forward amount of £50)

Expenditure

7	8	9	10	11	12	13	14	15	16
Date	Detail	Cash Spent	Cash to Bank	Bank Payments	Materials	Phone + Postage	Motor Expenses	Misc	Bank Deposits
	Bank Balance B/F								100 00
Dec 1	Banking		75 00						75 00
1	Petrol	10 00					10 00		
8	Telephone			29 50		29 50			
12	J Smith (materials)			62 75	62 75				
14	Postage Stamps	6 25				6 25			
14	Banking		100 00						100 00
15	Stationery	3 40						3 40	
15	Jones (materials)			16 50	16 50				
16	Banking		97 50						97 50
16	Bank Charges			6 25				6 25	
18	Banking		125 00						125 00
23	Owners' Drawings			100 00				100 00	
23	Banking		20 00						20 00
	Column Totals	19 65	417 50	215 00	79 25	35 75	10 00	109 65	417 50

652.15

652.15

Cross Casting this Month's Expenditure
(Excluding brought forward amount of £100)

33

Cross Casting the Totals

It is important to check the additions. On the income side, the total of columns 3 and 4 must equal the total of columns 5 and 6 (in our example, they both add up to £457.50).

On the expenditure side, the total of columns 9 to 11 must equal the total of columns 12 to 16 (in our example they both add up to £652.15). By checking these totals, you will know that your additions are correct. This is called cross casting. We all make mistakes in our book-keeping, cross casting eliminates many of these errors. It is important to do this before you attempt to reconcile the cash and bank (see later). This will save a lot of wasted time trying to reconcile figures which contain arithmetical mistakes.

Once we have cross cast the totals, we can check that the balances shown in our books agree with:

- the cash in the till and
- the cash in the bank.

This process is called reconciliation. We need to reconcile both the cash balance and the bank balance. If we can reconcile our books, we will have accounted for all of the money passing through the business. The following paragraphs show you how to do this.

Handy Tip When you write up your own records, begin each month on a new page. This will leave room for further entries which you may need to add after checking your bank statement.

Reconciling the Cash

At the end of every month, you will have a series of book-keeping entries and some cash and cheques left 'in the till'. How do we know whether this balance is correct? We need some way of reconciling the cash and cheques 'in hand' with the book-keeping entries for the month.

In our example, we told you that David and Jean brought forward a balance of £50 from the previous month. When they checked the till at the end of the month, they found they had a closing balance of £70.35. We can now check whether this amount is correct by doing the following calculation:

Reconciling the Cash!

		£
	Cash/cheques in hand b/fwd from November	50.00
Add	Cash received	40.00 (column 3)
		90.00
Less	Cash spent	19.65 (column 9)
	Cash/cheques in hand c/fwd to January	70.35

In this instance, David and Jean's books balanced. If the books didn't balance, they would have probably made one or more of the following mistakes.

- Someone has paid out cash without any entry appearing in the 'books'.
- Someone has received cash without an entry appearing in the 'books'.
- The entries in the cashbook have been copied down wrongly. This is why you cross cast your columns before cash reconciliation – it helps to get rid of arithmetical errors.
- Giving and receiving the wrong change.

If they hadn't found any mistakes or omissions to account for the discrepancy, it may have been caused by theft.

If the reason for the difference cannot be found, it is important to adjust the cashbook with an 'error' entry to reflect the actual amount of cash 'in the till'. If you don't adjust this month's cashbook entries then your cashbook won't balance next time either! Obviously, you hope you don't need to make many of these corrections as it shows that cash handling is out of control. In this case, you may need to smarten up your cash controls!

Reconciling the Bank Account

Why do I Need to Reconcile the Bank Account?

Reconciling the bank statement with the cashbook ensures that you can account for the different amounts shown on your bank statement and the amounts shown in your cashbook. Differences usually arise because:

- The bank statement shows entries not in your cashbook, eg
  - bank charges
  - direct debits that you have forgotten to enter in your cashbook
  - bank automated clearing service (BACS) payments into your account for which you have had no notification
  - bank mispostings.

- Your cashbook could show entries not in your bank account. Normally these will be unpresented cheques or deposits made into the bank too late in the day to appear on the bank statement.

Reconciling the Bank

- Mistaken entries in your cashbook (eg transposing entries in the cashbook). This is why you should cross cast your columns before doing a bank reconciliation. Cross casting takes out the silly arithmetical mistakes. This will save time later when you come to reconcile the bank.

The Bank Reconciliation

The bank is easy to reconcile because you have a bank statement to check your cashbook entries against.

When David and Jean added up all the banking entries in their cashbook, they calculated that they should have £302.50 in the bank calculated as follows:

		£
	Bank balance b/fwd from November	100.00 (given)
Add	Bank deposits (column 16)	417.50
		517.50
Less	Bank payments (column 11)	215.00
	Bank balance as per cashbook	302.50

Unfortunately, when David and Jean's bank statement arrived, it showed a balance of £382.50 as shown on page 38. How can the bank balance shown in the cashbook be reconciled with the bank balance shown on the bank statement?

Bank Statement – David and Jean Furniture

Date	Particulars	Payments £	Receipts £	Balance £
Dec 1	Opening Balance			100.00
Dec 1	Sundry credit		75.00	175.00
Dec 11	British Telecom	29.50		145.50
Dec 14	Sundry credit		100.00	245.50
Dec 15	J Smith	62.75		182.75
Dec 16	Sundry credit		97.50	280.25
Dec 16	Bank charges	6.25		274.00
Dec 18	Jones	16.50		257.50
Dec 18	Sundry credit		125.00	382.50
	Closing Balance c/fwd			382.50

When they ticked back the bank statement against the cashbook, they discovered that there were two extra entries in the cashbook which did not appear in the bank statement. These were £100 drawings on 23 December and £20.00 bankings also on 23 December.

To reconcile the two sets of figures, they need to adjust the bank statement to take account of these two outstanding items shown in the cashbook. Here is David and Jean's bank reconciliation for December:

Bank Reconciliation for 23 December

		£
	Bank balance per statement at 18 December	382.50
Add	Afterdate banking	20.00
		402.50
Less	Afterdate cheque	100.00
	Bank balance as per cashbook (c/fwd to January)	302.50

The cashbook shows the 'true' bank balance so the balance of £302.50 is carried forward to open next month's book-keeping entries.

Balancing the Books

Balancing the books is a neat way to *demonstrate* that all of the money coming into the business in the month has been accounted for. Balancing the books is nothing new; it simply pulls together all the information collected in the example so far and summarises it at the bottom of the page.

Have a look at page 40. We start by adding the cash balance carried forward (£70.35) to the bottom of column 9. We then add the reconciled bank balance carried forward as per the cashbook (£302.50) to the bottom of column 11. We can use these figures to demonstrate that we have balanced the cash and the bank.

Balancing the Cash

We can now account for all of the cash moving through the business. The totals of columns 3 and 4 (including the cash brought forward) represents all the money coming into the business.

The totals of columns 9 and 10 (including the cash carried forward) represent the total amount leaving the the business. Or, to put it another way:

Cash Balance b/fwd + Cash Income in Month	*must* ⟷ *equal*	Cash Expenditure + Cash Banked + Cash Balance c/fwd

If these totals balance then we can account for all cash received and spent. Notice that in our example the figures balance at £507.50.

David and Jean

December 19xx

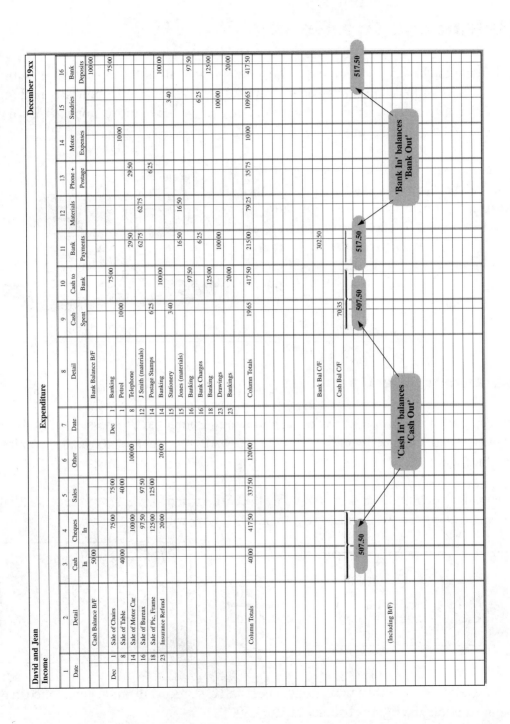

Income

1 Date	2 Detail	3 Cash In	4 Cheques In	5 Sales	6 Other
	Cash Balance B/F	50 00			
Dec 1	Sale of Chairs		75 00	75 00	
Dec 8	Sale of Table	40 00		40 00	
Dec 14	Sale of Motor Car		100 00		100 00
Dec 16	Sale of Bureax		97 50	97 50	
Dec 18	Sale of Pic. Frame		125 00	125 00	
Dec 23	Insurance Refund		20 00		20 00
	Column Totals	40 00	417 50	337 50	120 00
	(Including B/F)				

Expenditure

7 Date	8 Detail	9 Cash Spent	10 Cash to Bank	11 Bank Payments	12 Materials	13 Phone + Postage	14 Motor Expenses	15 Sundries	16 Bank Deposits
	Bank Balance B/F								100 00
Dec 1	Banking		75 00						75 00
Dec 1	Petrol	10 00					10 00		
Dec 8	Telephone			29 50		29 50			
Dec 12	J Smith (materials)			62 75	62 75				
Dec 14	Postage Stamps	6 25				6 25			
Dec 14	Banking		100 00						100 00
Dec 15	Stationery	3 40						3 40	
Dec 15	Jones (materials)			16 50	16 50				
Dec 16	Banking		97 50						97 50
Dec 16	Bank Charges			6 25				6 25	
Dec 18	Banking		125 00						125 00
Dec 18	Drawings			100 00				100 00	
Dec 23	Banking		20 00						20 00
Dec 23	Bankings								
	Column Totals	19 65	417 50	215 00	79 25	35 75	10 00	109 65	417 50
	Bank Bal C/F			302 50					517 50
	Cash Bal C/F	70 35	507 50	517 50					

Callouts:
- 'Cash In' balances 'Cash Out' — 507.50
- 'Bank In' balances 'Bank Out' — 517.50
- 507.50
- 517.50

Balancing the Bank

By the same token, the total of column 16 (including the brought forward amount) must equal the total of column 11 (including the carry forward amount). Or, to put it another way:

Bank Balance b/fwd + Bankings in the Month	must equal	Bank Payments + Bank Balance c/fwd

If these totals balance then we can account for all money moving through the bank. Notice that in our example the figures balance at £517.50.

David and Jean Exercise

Why not have a go at the following exercise yourself. Write up the cashbook for the next month which is January.

When you have completed this exercise, you will be able to:

- enter receipts
- enter payments
- cross cast the totals
- reconcile the cash
- reconcile the bank
- balance the books.

Exercise 2 – Making the entries

In the previous example, we balanced the cashbook at 23 December. No more entries were made over the Christmas period. This exercise will follow on and you can write up the cashbook for January.

Enter the income and expenditure amounts given below onto pages 44 and 45. Analyse both income and expenditure into the appropriate columns. You may remember the cash balance brought forward is £70.35. The bank balance brought forward is £302.50. When you have done this, proceed to Exercise 3. Check your answer with page 158.

Income

		£	
Jan 2	Sold – table	162.50	cheque banked Jan 6
5	Sold – settee	142.25	cheque banked Jan 6
10	Sold – book shelves	235.00	cheque banked Jan 11
14	Sold – timber	40.00	cash – used for expenses
19	Capital introduced	400.00	cheque banked Jan 19
19	Sold – bookcase	85.00	cheque banked Jan 19
27	Sold – desk	421.00	cheque banked Jan 30
28	Sold – old clock	190.00	cheque banked Jan 30

Payments

		£	
Jan 2	Postage stamps	8.00	paid cash
6	T Jones – materials	140.00	cheque
6	Banking	304.75	
10	S Roberts – materials	259.00	cheque
11	Banking	235.00	
14	Petrol	25.00	cash
19	Banking	485.00	
20	Rates	523.64	cheque
20	Electricity	98.33	cheque
20	Gas	204.25	cheque
22	Tea and coffee	4.74	cash
30	Banking	611.00	
30	Drawings – personal	300.00	cheque
30	Stationery	1.33	cash

Exercise 3 – Cross casting your totals

- Add up all the columns for 'income' and check that the total for columns 3 and 4 equals the total of columns 5 and 6.

- Add up all the columns on the payments side. The total of columns 9, 10 and 11 should equal the total of columns 12 to 16.

Check your answer with page 159.

Exercise 4 – Reconciling the cash

Remember the balance of cash in hand at 23 December was £70.35. Fill in the cash pro-forma set out below:

Cash Control

	£
Cash balance b/fwd from Dec	70.35
Add Cash received per cashbook	_____
Total	. . . . .
Less Cash payments per cashbook	_____
Cash balance c/fwd to Feb	_____

Here's a clue, the closing cash balance should be £71.28.

Check your answer with page 159.

David and Jean									
Income									
1	2	3		4		5		6	
Date	Detail	Cash In		Cheques In		Sales		Other	

January 19xx									
Expenditure									
7	8	9	10	11	12	13	14	15	16
Date	Detail	Cash Spent	Cash to Bank	Bank Payments	Materials	Phone + Postage	Motor Expenses	Sundries	Bank Deposits

Exercise 5 – Reconciling the bank

David and Jean received their bank statement and this is how it looked:

Bank Statement – David and Jean Furniture

Date	Particulars	Payments £	Receipts £	Balance £
18 Dec	Opening Balance			382.50
23 Dec	Drawings	100.00		282.50
23 Dec	Sundry credit		20.00	302.50
6 Jan	Sundry credit		304.75	607.25
9 Jan	T Jones	140.00		467.25
11 Jan	Sundry credit		235.00	702.25
13 Jan	S Roberts	259.00		443.25
19 Jan	Sundry credit		485.00	928.25
24 Jan	Rates	523.64		404.61
24 Jan	Electricity	98.33		306.28
24 Jan	Gas	204.25		102.03
	Closing Balance c/fwd			102.03

We are going to reconcile this bank statement part way through a month. Although most people reconcile the bank account at month end, you can do the reconciliation at any time convenient to yourself.

If you tick the bank statement back against the cashbook, you will find two entries in the cashbook which do not appear on the bank statement. What are they?

Exercise 5 (contd)

You will see that the balance on the bank statement of £102.03 does not agree with the bank balance carried forward in the cashbook which is £413.03. Can you reconcile the cashbook and bank statement using the following pro-forma? Check your answers with page 160.

Bank Reconciliation at 24 January

		£
	Balance per statement 24 January	102.03
Add	Unrecorded afterdate bankings	_____
	Total	. . . . .
Less	Unpresented cheques for payments out	_____
	Bank balance c/fwd per cashbook	413.03

A Bank Reconciliation?

You have now completed your book-keeping! Have you balanced the books? If not, review your figures; it is possible that you have entered your opening and closing balances the wrong way round. Check your answers with those given on pages 159 and 160.

A Note on Handling Cash

We have shown cheques and cash recorded separately into columns 3 and 4. In practice, most businesses would not go to this level of detail. Most businesses simply lump together all money collected into a single column. This is a very good idea especially if you bank the *whole* of the daily takings intact. Banking intact has important benefits for the business.

- It avoids cash lying around the business which is an invitation to theft by employees and intruders.

- If you bank the whole of the takings intact, you will have *evidence* of income. This evidence will be valuable if you have a VAT or Inland Revenue audit. You will also be able to satisfy your professional auditor that you have recorded income correctly. Under-recording of income is tempting, but it is a serious (and often detectable) offence.

- If you pay bills with cash from the till, you may forget to get a receipt. This means that you have no evidence of expenditure – which could be used to cut your VAT liability and your profit tax liability.

- Owners of small businesses sometimes take their drawings from cash in the till. This can be an open invitation for employees to 'borrow' money also.

Of course, you don't want to pay for small expenditures by cheque. This would increase your bank charges enormously. We suggest you restrict cash payments to petty cash using the routine recommended in Chapter 8.

In the next chapter, we will demonstrate the flexibility of the analysed cashbook by incorporating the changes suggested above.

Chapter 4

Book-keeping for 'Cash Accounting' Traders

In this chapter, we will introduce two modifications to the analysed cashbook shown in the previous chapter. These cover:

- VAT under the cash accounting scheme

- the changes to cash handling outlined at the end of the previous chapter.

Cash Accounting

You are allowed to account for VAT using the 'cash accounting' method providing that your taxable turnover doesn't exceed the cash accounting limit. At the time of writing these notes, the limit for cash accounting was £437,500 of taxable turnover.

Cash Accounting!

If the taxable turnover exceeds the cash accounting limit, you have no choice but to account for VAT based on the tax point date. Chapter 6 explains how to keep books using tax point accounting.

Cash accounting is generally advantageous to the trader because:

- it is simple to operate
- it provides automatic VAT relief for bad debt
- it can offer some traders a cash flow advantage.

'Cash accounting' is not, of course, just confined to notes and coins. Cash in this context includes all forms of money changing hands whether cash, cheques, credit cards etc.

Under cash accounting rules, VAT is accounted for according to the *date when cash is received or paid.* This means, for example, that if a customer pays you three months late then you only have to account for the value added tax at the time that you actually receive the money.

Book-keeping entries for traders on cash accounting are similar to those used by non-registered traders with one exception. An extra column for VAT is added on both the income and the expenditure sides. We need this extra column because the books now serve two purposes. These are:

- to provide VAT records, which will be used to complete your quarterly VAT return, *and*

- to produce book-keeping entries (net of VAT) that keep you informed about the day-to-day progress of the business. They will also be used by your accountant when he/she prepares your annual accounts for submission to the Inland Revenue.

Changes in Cash Handling

We mentioned at the end of Chapter 3 that it is good business practice to bank the whole of your takings intact. If you do this, there is little point in maintaining separate income columns for cash and bank as we did in the David and Jean example in Chapter 3. We will now enter all income in the 'total income' column (see column 3 on page 57).

Since we bank our takings intact, we won't be able to use cash out of the till to pay for expenses. We now pay for expenses in one of two ways:

- by cheque if the expense is large
- from petty cash if the expense is small.

Petty cash is dealt with in detail in Chapter 8. For the moment, we will simply accept that small expenses are paid from a petty cash box which is topped up periodically by drawing money from the bank. Since we are not spending cash *from the till*, we can now eliminate the 'cash out' column (which was column 9 in the David and Jean example).

This alternative layout demonstrates one of the main benefits of the analysed cashbook. It can be modified to fit any type of business.

Example

To illustrate how cash accounting works, we have taken an imaginary business owned by Mr Hardcastle. He trades as a hardware store supplying goods to builders and DIY customers.

Hardcastle's Hardware Shop

We will use Mr Hardcastle's business to demonstrate:

- recording income
- recording expenditure
- cross casting the income and expenditure totals
- reconciling the cash
- reconciling the bank
- balancing the books
- completing the VAT return.

Recording Receipts

Mr Hardcastle had the following receipts for January.

Date	Transaction	Sales (incl VAT)	Other Income (not VATable)
		£	£
Jan 1	Sales	223.65	
1	Sales	235.00	
2	Sales	354.74	
6	Sales	124.32	
6	Capital introduced		1000.00
10	Sales	294.89	
12	Sales	264.33	
15	Sales	324.78	
15	Sales	110.66	
18	Sales	142.56	
19	Sales	210.45	
21	Sales	189.46	
21	Sales	88.44	
25	Sales	110.69	
27	Sales	224.52	
30	Sales	145.96	
	Total	**3044.45**	**1000.00**

Notice that Mr Hardcastle has kept 'sales' and
'other income' quite separate. 'Other income'
comprises everything except sales (like a bank
loan, interest received on bank deposits, or sale
of assets like an old car, or machine).

Notice also that all of the sales figures
include value added tax. We will need to
extract the VAT element when we enter
these figures in our 'books'.

Recording Receipts

See how these entries are recorded below. Note
that VAT has been extracted from the receipts
using the VAT fraction calculated in Chapter 2. You may remember that the VAT
fraction for the 17½% rate of VAT is 7/47.

Income

1 Date		2 Detail	3 Total Income		4 VAT		5 Sales		6 Other Income		
Jan	1	Sales	223	65	33	31	190	34			
	1	Sales	235	00	35	00	200	00			
	2	Sales	354	74	52	83	301	91			
	6	Sales	124	32	18	52	105	80			
	6	Capital Introduced	1000	00					1000	00	
	10	Sales	294	89	43	92	250	97			
	12	Sales	264	33	39	37	224	96			
	15	Sales	324	78	48	37	276	41			
	15	Sales	110	66	16	48	94	18			
	18	Sales	142	56	21	23	121	33			
	19	Sales	210	45	31	34	179	11			
	21	Sales	189	46	28	22	161	24			
	21	Sales	88	44	13	17	75	27			
	25	Sales	110	69	16	49	94	20			
	27	Sales	224	52	33	44	191	08			
	30	Sales	145	96	21	74	124	22			
		Totals	4044	45	453	43	2591	02	1000	00	

We have recorded these figures, together with a cash balance brought forward of £50,
on page 57.

Recording Payments

Mr Hardcastle made the following payments and bankings.

Date	Transaction	Amount £	Comment
Jan 1	J Brown (stock)	423.46	cheque
2	Banking	458.65	
6	Banking	354.74	
6	Wages	124.65	cheque
10	British Telecom	84.56	cheque
10	F Robinson (stock)	224.47	cheque
10	Banking	1124.32	
10	Banking	294.89	
12	Banking	264.33	
15	Banking	435.44	
18	Electricity	154.58	cheque (VAT at 17½%)
18	Banking	142.56	
19	Bank charges	20.00	direct charge
19	Banking	210.45	
25	F Jones (stock)	445.98	cheque
25	Banking	277.90	
27	Rates	564.12	cheque
27	Banking	110.69	
29	Bluett (stock)	324.58	cheque
29	Banking	224.52	
30	Banking	145.96	

In addition, the following payments were met from petty cash.

Jan 1	Petrol	20.00
6	Stationery	24.65
12	Postage*	5.45
15	Tea and Coffee**	8.65
25	Petrol	25.00
29	Petrol	25.00
	Total	**108.75**

* Postage is VAT exempt ** Tea and coffee are zero rated

The petty cash box was topped up on 30 Jan with the total sum of £108.75.

We will now break this expenditure down into columns. We will record:

- how much money was spent
- how much income was banked
- where the money has gone (eg wages, materials, etc)
- how much VAT was paid out.

The last point is important – we need to record VAT so that we can offset the VAT paid out against the VAT collected on sales. Remember that any VAT surplus collected by the business does not belong to the business, it belongs to Customs and Excise.

Here is how we would record these expenditures. Why not tick back the payments on page 544 against the entries below checking that you agree each one as you go?

Expenditure

8 Date	9 Detail	10 To Bank	11 Bank Payments	12 VAT	13 Materials	14 Travel + Petrol	15 Telephone	16 Light + Heat	17 Printing Stationery	18 Wages	19 Sundries	20 Bankings
Jan 1	J Brown (stock)		423 46	63 07	360 39							
2	Banking	458 65										458 65
6	Banking	354 74										354 74
6	Wages		124 65							124 65		
10	B Telecom		84 56	12 59			71 97					
10	F Robinson (stock)		224 47	33 43	191 04							
10	Banking	1124 32										1124 32
10	Banking	294 89										294 89
12	Banking	264 33										264 33
15	Banking	435 44										435 44
18	Electricity		154 58	23 02				131 56				
18	Banking	142 56										142 56
19	Bank charges		20 00								20 00	
19	Banking	210 45										210 45
25	F Jones (stock)		445 98	66 42	379 56							
25	Banking	277 90										277 90
27	Rates		564 12								564 12	
27	Banking	110 69										110 69
29	Bluett (stock)		324 58	48 34	276 24							
29	Banking	224 52										224 52
30	Banking	145 96										145 96
30	Petty cash		108 75	14 09		59 58			20 98		14 10	
	Totals	4044 45	2475 15	260 96	1207 23	59 58	71 97	131 56	20 98	124 65	598 22	4044 45

We have entered these figures together with a bank balance brought forward of £500.25 on page 57.

Cross Casting the Totals

Cross Casting the Income Totals

Notice on page 57 how the columns have been added up and cross cast. On the income side, the totals of columns 4, 5 and 6 must add up to the total in column 3, ie:

			£	£
Column	3	**Total Income**		**4044.45**
Column	4	VAT	453.43	
Column	5	Cash sales	2591.02	
Column	6	Other Income	1000.00	
Total Columns 4–6				**4044.45**

Everyone makes mistakes with their entries and additions. 'Cross casting' the totals helps to eliminate these mistakes.

Cross Casting the Totals

Cross Casting the Expenditure Totals

Notice on page 57 how the totals of columns 10 and 11 add up to the totals of columns 12–20 viz:

			£	£
Column	10	To Bank	4044.45	
Column	11	Total payments	2475.15	
Total Columns		**10 and 11**		**6519.60**
Column	12	VAT	260.96	
Column	13	Materials	1207.23	
Column	14	Travel/motor	59.58	
Column	15	Telephone	71.97	
Column	16	Light & heat	131.56	
Column	17	Printing & stationery	20.98	
Column	18	Wages	124.65	
Column	19	Sundries	598.22	
Column	20	Bankings	4044.45	
Total Columns		**12–20**		**6519.60**

Hardcastle's Hardware — January 19xx

Income

1 Date	2 Detail	3 Total In	4 VAT	5 Sales	6 Other Income	7
	Cash b/fwd	50 00				
Jan 1	Sales	223 65	33 31	190 34		
1	Sales	235 00	35 00	200 00		
2	Sales	354 74	52 83	301 91		
6	Sales	124 32	18 52	105 80		
6	Capital Introduced	1000 00			1000 00	
10	Sales	294 89	43 92	250 97		
12	Sales	264 33	39 37	224 96		
15	Sales	324 78	48 37	276 41		
15	Sales	110 66	16 48	94 18		
18	Sales	142 56	21 23	121 33		
19	Sales	210 45	31 34	179 11		
21	Sales	189 46	28 22	161 24		
21	Sales	88 44	13 17	75 27		
25	Sales	110 69	16 49	94 20		
27	Sales	224 52	33 44	191 08		
30	Sales	145 96	21 74	124 22		
	Column Totals	4044 45	453 43	2591 02	1000 00	

£4044.45

Expenditure

8 Date	9 Detail	10 To Bank	11 Bank Payments	12 VAT	13 Materials	14 Travel + Petrol	15 Telephone	16 Light Heat	17 Printing Stationery	18 Wages	19 Sundries	20 Bankings
	Bank Balance B/F											500 25
Jan 1	J Brown (stock)		423 46	63 07	360 39							
2	Banking	458 65										458 65
6	Banking	354 74										354 74
6	Wages		124 65							124 65		
10	B Telecom		84 56	12 59			71 97					
10	F Robinson (stock)		224 47	33 43	191 04							
10	Banking	1124 32										1124 32
12	Banking	294 89										294 89
15	Banking	264 33										264 33
18	Banking	435 44										435 44
18	Electricity		154 58	23 02				131 56				
19	Banking	142 56										142 56
19	Bank charges		20 00								20 00	
19	Banking	210 45										210 45
25	F Jones (stock)		445 98	66 42	379 56							
25	Banking	277 90										277 90
27	Rates		564 12								564 12	
27	Banking	110 69										110 69
29	Bluett (stock)		324 58	48 34	276 24							
29	Banking	224 52										224 52
30	Banking	145 96										145 96
30	Petty cash		108 75	14 09		59 58			20 98		14 10	
	Column Totals	4044 45	2475 15	260 96	1207 23	59 58	71 97	131 56	20 98	124 65	598 22	4044 45

£6519.60

£6519.60

Reconciling the Cash

Although this paragraph is called reconciling the cash, we are actually trying to reconcile the total money coming into the business (column 3) with the total money going out of the business (column 10). Since we bank *all* of the cash received, the two totals should, obviously, be the same. This means we should end the month with the same 'float' as we started the month.

In Mr Hardcastle's case, he opened January with £50 cash in hand. This means that his closing cash balance must also be £50, calculated as follows:

		£
	Opening Cash Balance b/fwd	50.00
Add	Cash In	4044.45 (column 3)
		4094.45
Less	Cash Out	4044.45 (column 10)
	Closing Cash Balance c/fwd	50.00

Of course, if the till does indeed contain £50 then everything is fine. If, however, the till does not contain £50, we need to do some detective work. For example:

- have all the entries in the cashbook been entered correctly?
- were the banking slips completed correctly?
- was the opening balance figure brought forward from the last month correctly?
- is the arithmetic correct?
- has anyone 'borrowed' any money?
- can anyone remember anything happening which may have caused the mistake?

Notice how easy it is to reconcile 'cash' if you bank your takings intact. If all of your money ends up in the bank, the only cash left to reconcile is that left in the till at the end of the month waiting to be deposited in the bank next month.

Reconciled!

Reconciling the Bank Account

Why do I Need to Reconcile the Bank Account?

Reconciling the bank account ensures that you have the same amount of money shown on your bank statement as you have in your cashbook. You may remember from Chapter 3 that differences can arise because:

- The bank account shows entries not in your cashbook, eg
  - bank charges
  - direct debits which you have forgotten to enter in your cashbook
  - bank automated clearing service (BACS) payments into your account for which you have no notification
  - bank mispostings.

- Your cashbook shows entries not in your bank account. Normally these will be unpresented cheques or payments into the bank made too late in the day to appear on that day's bank statement.

- Mistaken entries by you, eg transposing entries in the cashbook or simply copying wrong numbers into your cashbook. This is why you should cross cast your columns before doing a bank reconciliation. Cross casting takes out the silly arithmetical mistakes. This will save time when you come to reconcile the bank.

The bank is easier to balance because you have a bank statement to check your banking entries against.

Let's look at Mr Hardcastle's bank statement for the month of January on page 60.

We can now reconcile Mr Hardcastle's bank balance with the cashbook on page 57.

The balance on the cashbook is calculated as:

		£	
	Reconciled Bank Balance b/fwd	500.25	(b/fwd from Dec – given)
Add	Bankings	4044.45	(column 20)
Less	Bank Payments	2475.15	(column 11)
	Bank Balance per cashbook c/fwd	2069.55	

Bank Statement - Hardcastle's Hardware

Date	Particulars	Payments £	Receipts £	Balance £
Jan 1	Opening Balance			500.25
2	Sundry Credit		458.65	958.90
6	Sundry Credit		354.74	1313.64
6	J Brown	423.46		890.18
9	Wages	124.65		765.53
10	Sundry Credit		1124.32	1889.85
10	Sundry Credit		294.89	2184.74
13	F Robinson	224.47		1960.27
13	British Telecom	84.56		1875.71
13	Sundry Credit		264.33	2140.04
15	Sundry Credit		435.44	2575.48
18	Sundry Credit		142.56	2718.04
19	Bank Charges	20.00		2698.04
19	Sundry Credit		210.45	2908.49
21	Electricity	154.58		2753.91
25	Sundry Credit		277.90	3031.81
28	Sundry Credit		110.69	3142.50
	Closing Balance c/fwd			3142.50

If you tick the cashbook entries back against the bank statement, you will find that there are six entries in the cashbook which do not appear on the bank statement.

These are:

		£
29 Jan	Banking	224.52
30 Jan	Banking	145.96
25 Jan	F Jones	445.98
27 Jan	Rates	564.12
29 Jan	Bluett	324.58
30 Jan	Petty Cash	108.75

If we include these six entries which are in the cashbook but not in the bank, we have:

Bank Reconciliation at 31 January

		£	£
Balance per Statement at 31 January			3142.50
Add Bankings not recorded			
	Jan 29	224.52	
	Jan 30	145.96	
			370.48
			3512.98
Less Unpresented cheques for payments out			
	Jan 25	445.98	
	Jan 27	564.12	
	Jan 30	324.58	
	Jan 30	108.75	
			1443.43
Bank Balance per Cashbook C/fwd			2069.55

You can now see that the bank statement is reconciled with the closing balance in the cashbook.

As a matter of interest, we would find that our *next* bank statement, ie that for February, would probably start with the items missing from the end of this month's statement. We have marked these items with an asterisk.

Bank Statement – Hardcastle's Hardware				
Date	Particulars	Payments £	Receipts £	Balance £
Feb 1	Opening balance			3142.50
*Feb 1	To cash	108.75		3033.75
*Feb 1	Sundry credit		224.52	3258.27
*Feb 1	Sundry credit		145.96	3404.23
*Feb 1	F Jones	445.98		2958.25
*Feb 2	Rates	564.12		2394.13
*Feb 3	Bluett	324.58		2069.55

Notice that the balance partway through the February statement comes to the same value as the cashbook, ie £2,069.55. This is because the missing items from the previous bank reconciliation have now had time to find their way through the banking system.

Look at page 63. You will see that we have entered the bank balance brought forward from December (which is £500.25) at the top of column 20. We have also entered the bank balance carried forward to February (which is £2,069.55) towards the bottom of column 11. We will use these totals in the next section which is called 'Balancing the Books'.

Balancing the Books

This is the final stage of book-keeping. It pulls together all the work undertaken so far and presents it on one sheet of paper. It proves that we have done a thorough job of the month's records.

Look at page 63. Notice that there are four boxes shown on the bottom of the page. These are labelled 'Balancing the Cash' and 'Balancing the Bank'. If both 'Balancing the Cash' boxes agree, you can be pretty sure that you have got your cash right. Likewise, if both 'Balancing the Bank' boxes balance, you should have no trouble with your bank records.

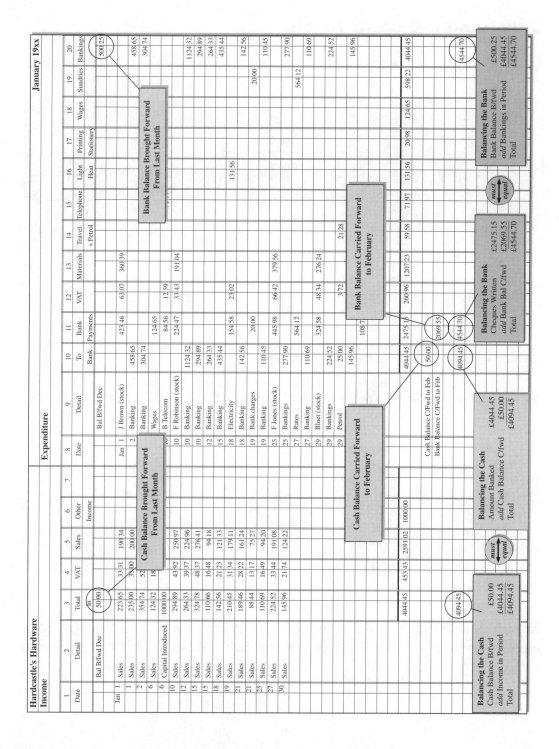

Balancing the Cash Totals

If you think about **cash** for the moment, the following relationship must hold true.

Cash Balance b/fwd (£50) + Cash/Cheques/etc rec'd in month (£4,044.45)		Cash/Cheques/etc Banked (£4,044.45) + Cash Balance c/fwd (£50)

Look on the bottom left of page 63 at the two boxes labelled 'Balancing the Cash'. We have inserted the appropriate cash balances into each box. Since both add up to the same amount, we have 'balanced our cash'.

Balancing the Bank Totals

By the same token, the following relationships must hold good for our dealings with the bank.

Bank Balance b/fwd (£500.25) + Banking in the month (£4,044.45)		Cheques etc written (£2,475.15) + Bank Balance c/fwd (£2,069.55)

Notice that we have included these two boxes on page 63 with the appropriate figures inserted. The boxes are labelled 'Balancing the Bank'. Again the numbers balance so we have 'balanced the bank'.

Completing the VAT Return

Let's have a go at completing the VAT return on page 66 for Mr Hardcastle's business using VAT form 100. We will need information taken from page 63.

Normally, of course, we would base the VAT return on a quarter's figures. However, since we don't have a quarter's figures, we will base the VAT return on January's figures alone. This is how you fill in the boxes on your VAT return.

Box 1

This is the total VAT due on sales (output tax). It is taken from column 4 of the cashbook. If you use your car for business and private use and wish to reclaim VAT on motoring expenses, you must add the scale charge into this box.

Box 3

Enter the total of box 1 and box 2. In our example, there are no entries in box 2 so enter the same figure as box 1.

Box 4

Enter the total VAT paid on purchases (input VAT). This is taken from column 12 in our cashbook.

Box 5

Enter here the difference between box 3 (output tax) and box 4 (input tax). The result is the amount you owe HMC&E.

Box 6

Enter here the total taxable sales net of VAT. This is the sum of column 5. Inputs and outputs are entered as whole pounds on the VAT return. You need to adjust this figure for the VAT scale charge on motoring expenses, if applicable (see page 67 for more detail on scale charges).

Box 7

Enter here the total value of purchases and other inputs excluding any VAT. This is the sum of columns 13 to 17 and column 19, excluding bank charges of £20 and business rates of £564 that are outside the scope of VAT.

Value Added Tax Return

For the period

For Official Use

HM Customs
and Excise

Registration Number

Period

You could be liable to a financial penalty it your completed return and all the VAT payable are not received by the due date.

Due date:

For
Official
Use

Your VAT Office telephone number is

Before you fill in this form please read the notes on the back and the VAT leaflet *"Filling in your VAT return".* Fill in all boxes clearly in ink, and write 'none' where necessary. Don't put a dash or leave any box blank. If there are no pence write **"00"** in the pence column. **Do not** enter more than one amount in any box.

		£	p
For official use	VAT due in this period on **sales** and other outputs	1	453	43
	VAT due in this period on **acquisitions** from other **EC Member States**	2	None	
	Total VAT due **(the sum of boxes 1 and 2)**	3	453	43
	VAT reclaimed in this period on **purchases** and other inputs (including acquisitions from the EC)	4	260	96
	Net VAT to be paid to Customs or reclaimed by you **(Difference between boxes 3 and 4)**	5	192	47
	Total value of **sales** and all other outputs excluding any VAT. **Include your box 8 figure**	6	2591	00
	Total value of **purchases** and all other inputs excluding any VAT. **Include your box 9 figure**	7	1505	00
	Total value of all **supplies** of goods and related services, excluding any VAT, to other **EC Member States**	8	None	00
	Total value of all **acquisitions** of goods and related services, excluding any VAT, from other **EC Member States**	9	None	00

Retail schemes. If you have used any of the schemes in the period covered by this return, enter the relevant letter(s) in this box.

If you are enclosing a payment please tick this box.

DECLARATION: You, or someone on your behalf, must sign below.

I,..declare that the
(Full name of signatory in BLOCK LETTERS)

information given above is true and complete.

Signature...Date.............19......

A false declaration can result in prosecution.

L

VAT 100

Fuel Scale Charges

In the Hardcastle example, we have simply included the values taken from the cashbook. However, you may have noticed that one of the items shown in the January cashbook was for petrol for which we have reclaimed value added tax. Assuming that the vehicle had private use then we should have added a scale charge for this vehicle. Here is an example of how the scale charge would be applied.

Example

Assume Mr Hardcastle has a 1900cc petrol vehicle used in the business which is also used privately. The unadjusted VAT return for the quarter showed the following figures.

Box 1   VAT due in this period on sales and other outputs   £453.43
Box 6   Total value of sales and all other outputs excl VAT   £2,591.00

Using the VAT scale charge shown on page 20, the figures would be adjusted as follows:

		£
Box 1	VAT Output Tax	453.43
	Add Scale Charge	39.91
	Revised box 1 figure	493.34
Box 6	VAT Outputs excluding VAT	2591.00
	Add Scale Charges	228.00 *
	Revised box 6 figure	2819.00

*   Remember to enter the figure net of VAT. In our case, this is VAT scale charge £268 less VAT £39.91 = £228 (rounding to nearest whole pound).

We have now finished the job, the books are cross cast. We have also been able to reconcile the cash and bank and we have completed the VAT return!

Exercise 6

Let's stay with Mr Hardcastle's business. Here is a set of exercises for you to try yourself. These figures relate to the following month which is February.

Entering Receipts

Complete the income side for Mr Hardcastle's business for February using the information given below. Use the blank form on pages 72 and 73 for your entries. Enter the date, description and total amount first. Then analyse the total across columns 4 to 7 exactly as we did for the previous month. Remember to calculate the VAT on sales at 7/47. The vehicle has been sold for £100 plus VAT of £17.50. The cash balance brought forward is £50.

Date		Description	Sales (incl VAT) £	Other Income (incl VAT) £
Feb	1	Sales	246.45	
	1	Sales	558.12	
	3	Sales	312.94	
	6	Sales	185.46	
	10	Sales	194.74	
	15	Sales	321.89	
	18	Sales	218.95	
	19	Sales	314.58	
	19	Sale of van		117.50
	22	Sales	134.58	
	24	Sales	215.69	

Continued

Exercise 6 (Contd)

Date	Description	Sales (incl VAT) £	Other Income (incl VAT) £
Feb 24	Sales	352.50	
25	Sales	216.78	
26	Sales	358.74	
28	Sales	421.64	
	Total	4053.06	117.50

If you are unsure whether you have done the exercise correctly, check your answers against the model on page 161.

Exercise 7 – Recording Payments

Enter the following payments on the right hand side of pages 72 and 73. Remember to enter the 'bankings' in the columns 10 and 20. Put the cheque payments in the bank payments column (col 11). Then analyse the expenditure into the other columns. The bank balance brought forward is £2,069.55. Remember to extract the VAT, where appropriate, which should be entered in the VAT column (col 12). If you have problems, check with the model answer on page 161.

Date	Transaction	Amount £	Paid By
Feb 1	Building supplies (stock)	423.65	Cheque
1	Acme Paint Co (stock)	258.96	Cheque
2	Wages	135.00	Cheque
3	Banking	246.45	
6	Banking	558.12	
6	Banking	312.94	

Continued overleaf

Exercise 7 (Contd)

Date	Transaction	Amount £	Paid By
Feb 10	Gas	125.94	Cheque (VAT @ 17½%)
10	Banking	185.46	
15	Banking	194.74	
15	Red Brick Co (stock)	321.65	Cheque
15	Telephone	81.05	Cheque
18	Bank Charges	20.00	Direct Debit
18	Banking	321.89	
19	Banking	218.95	
22	Banking	432.08	
24	Banking	134.58	
25	Banking	568.19	
25	The Hardware Co	824.23	Cheque
26	Mr Hardcastle's drawings	500.00	Cheque
26	Banking	216.78	
27	Banking	358.74	
28	Banking	421.64	
28	Petty cash top-up	72.32	

The following payments were made from petty cash this month.

2	Petrol	35.00	Petty cash
2	Stationery	12.36	Petty cash
10	Postage	5.00	Petty cash
24	Tea/coffee	4.96	Petty cash
27	Petrol	15.00	Petty cash
	Total petty cash for month	**72.32**	

Petty cash was topped up by drawing a cheque for £72.32 on 28 February.

Note All purchased items are standard rated, except postage and bank charges which are exempt. Tea and coffee are zero rated. Wages are outside the scope of VAT.

Exercise 8 – Cross Casting

- Add up all the income columns. Agree the total income (column 3) with the totals of columns 4 to 6.

- Agree the total of columns 10 and 11 with the totals of columns 12–20.

Check your answers with page 162.

Exercise 9 – Reconciling the Cash

Complete the cash reconciliation below, we have given you the opening cash balance.

	£
Cash in hand b/fwd from previous period	50.00
Add Income	
	_____
Less Payments	. . . . .
Cash in hand c/fwd to next period	_____
	_____

Check your answer with page 162.

Hardcastle's Hardware
Income

1	2	3	4	5	6	7
Date	Detail	Total In	VAT	Sales	Other Income	

Expenditure

8	9	10	11	12	13	14	15	16	17	18	19	20
Date	Detail	To Bank	Bank Payments	VAT	Materials	Travel + Petrol	Telephone	Light Heat	Printing Stationery	Wages	Sundries	Bankings

Exercise 10 – Reconciling the bank

Prepare a bank reconciliation using the bank statement shown below. The reconciliation period is 1 February to 28 February.

Bank Statement – Hardcastle's Hardware

Date	Particulars	Payments £	Receipts £	Balance £
Feb 1	Opening Balance			3142.50
1	To cash	108.75		3033.75
1	Sundry credit		224.52	3258.27
1	Sundry credit		145.96	3404.23
1	F Jones	445.98		2958.25
2	Rates	564.12		2394.13
3	Bluett	324.58		2069.50
3	Sundry credit		246.45	2316.00
4	Building Supplies	423.65		1892.35
4	Acme Paint Co	258.96		1633.39
5	Wages	135.00		1498.39
6	Sundry credit		558.12	2056.51
6	Sundry credit		312.94	2369.45
10	Sundry credit		185.46	2554.91
13	Gas	125.94		2428.97
15	Sundry credit		194.74	2623.71
18	Red Brick Co	321.65		2302.06
18	Telephone	81.05		2221.01
18	Bank charges	20.00		2201.01
18	Sundry credit		321.89	2522.90
19	Sundry credit		218.95	2741.85
22	Sundry credit		432.08	3173.93
24	Sundry credit		134.58	3308.51
25	Sundry credit		568.19	3876.70
26	Sundry credit		216.78	4093.48
27	Sundry credit		358.74	4452.22
28	The Hardware Co	824.23		3627.99
	Closing Balance c/fwd			3627.99

Exercise 10 (Contd)

Bank Balance per Cashbook

		£
	Reconciled bank balance b/fwd	2069.55
Add	Bank deposits	<u>4170.56</u>
		6240.11
Less	Bank payments	<u>2762.80</u>
	Closing balance c/fwd per cashbook	<u>3477.31</u>

Bank Reconciliation at 28 February

		£
	Balance per statement at 28 February	. . . . .
Add	Bankings not shown on statement	————
Less	Unpresented cheques	. . . . .
	Bank balance per cashbook c/fwd	————

Check your answer with page 163.

Exercise 11 – Completing the VAT Return

Normally the VAT return is completed on a quarterly basis. However, for illustration purposes, we will complete a VAT return using Mr Hardcastle's cashbook figures just for February. Mr Hardcastle has a 1900cc petrol vehicle used in his business which is also used for private motoring. We must, therefore, adjust the VAT return to include the scale charge. Normally, of course, we would use the quarterly scale charge as shown on page 20. However, for the purpose of this exercise, we will assume that one month's scale charge is £89 with VAT due of £13.25 (net of VAT scale charge rounded to £76). The following skeleton should help ensure that you take the right entries into account.

Calculation of VAT Due

	£	
Sales Output Tax	· · · · · · · ·	} (box 1)
VAT due per Car	· · · · · · · ·	
Purchases Input Tax	_____	(box 4)
Amount due to HMC&E	_____	(box 5)

Value of Sales Outputs
(rounded to nearest pound)

Cash Sales	· · · · · · · ·	
Net of VAT Scale Charges	· · · · · · · ·	
Credit Sales	· · · · · · · ·	
Sale of Van	_____	
Total	_____	(box 6)

Value of Purchase Inputs
(rounded to nearest pound)

Materials	· · · · · · · ·	
Travel/Motor	· · · · · · · ·	
Telephone	· · · · · · · ·	
Light and Heat	· · · · · · · ·	
Printing and Stationery	· · · · · · · ·	
Sundries/Post/Tea*	10.00	(see page 78)
Total	_____	(box 7)

Value Added Tax Return

HM Customs and Excise

For the period

Question 11 (Contd)

Your VAT Office telephone number is

For Official Use

Registration Number	Period

You could be liable to a financial penalty it your completed return and all the VAT payable are not received by the due date.

Due date:

For Official Use	

Before you fill in this form please read the notes on the back and the VAT leaflet *"Filling in your VAT return"*. Fill in all boxes clearly in ink, and write 'none' where necessary. Don't put a dash or leave any box blank. If there are no pence write **"00"** in the pence column. **Do not** enter more than one amount in any box.

For official use		£	p
VAT due in this period on **sales** and other outputs	1		
VAT due in this period on **acquisitions** from other **EC Member States**	2		
Total VAT due **(the sum of boxes 1 and 2)**	3		
VAT reclaimed in this period on **purchases** and other inputs (including acquisitions from the EC)	4		
Net VAT to be paid to Customs or reclaimed by you **(Difference between boxes 3 and 4)**	5		
Total value of **sales** and all other outputs excluding any VAT. **Include your box 8 figure**	6		00
Total value of **purchases** and all other inputs excluding any VAT. **Include your box 9 figure**	7		00
Total value of all **supplies** of goods and related services, excluding any VAT, to other **EC Member States**	8		00
Total value of all **acquisitions** of goods and related services, excluding any VAT, from other **EC Member States**	9		00

Retail schemes. If you have used any of the schemes in the period covered by this return, enter the relevant letter(s) in this box.

If you are enclosing a payment please tick this box.

DECLARATION: You, or someone on your behalf, must sign below.

I,...declare that the
(Full name of signatory in BLOCK LETTERS)

information given above is true and complete.

Signature...Date.............19......

A false declaration can result in prosecution.

L

VAT 100

*Note   We give you the value of £10 for this entry. The value included in box 7 includes both standard and zero rated and exempt items. Even though there is no VAT due on postage and tea/coffee (because they are exempt or zero rated), they must be included. Drawings and most bank charges are outside the scope of VAT and are, therefore, excluded.

You have now completed all the exercises. If you have made some mistakes, go over the entries again and correct them from the answers on pages 162 to 165.

Your own Book-keeping System

Of course, you may decide to use some of the headings shown on these examples for your own book-keeping system. However, don't slavishly copy down the column titles shown here. Choose items of income and expenditure which relate to your own type of business. Here are some tips.

Income

Normally, you won't have too many types of income. Some businesses simply split income between cash and credit sales (allocating one column to each). Alternatively, you could split income by type of income; for example, a hotel could have income columns for 'bar sales', 'meal sales' and 'accommodation'. This way you can see at a glance which business activities bring in the most revenue.

Expenditure

You will normally want more analysis columns on the expenditure side of the cashbook. This is because you want to know where your money is going. Obviously, you could have a column for every conceivable type of expenditure. However, this would make your cashbook a metre wide! In practice, you will normally find that around half a dozen columns will record over 80% of the money you spend. Typically these columns would comprise wages, materials, building occupancy costs, administration, transport, selling etc. Choose the half dozen items of expenditure that are large enough to warrant tracking in *your* book-keeping system. Dedicate a column to each. Be sure to leave one column for miscellaneous (or sundry) expenditure. Be careful, however, to label each item of miscellaneous expenditure clearly in the 'details' column. That way, if you need to find out how much you've spent on one particular miscellaneous item, it won't take long for you to scan the column and extract the figure that you are looking for.

Chapter 5

Computerised Book-keeping

Nowadays, many people are brought up with computers from an early age. To these people, entering numbers by hand into an analysis book seems distinctly old fashioned. Today's generation is well aware that the most efficient way to record numbers in rows and columns is with a computerised spreadsheet. For anyone unsure how a spreadsheet program works, here is a brief description.

Spreadsheets

Years before computers were invented, accountants were already collecting information onto sheets of paper called spreadsheets. Data was entered in rows and columns and many hours were spent calculating and recalculating spreadsheet numbers by hand. It is not surprising, therefore, that one of the earliest computer programs written for the personal computer (PC) was a spreadsheet program called Visicalc. The need for Visicalc drove early sales of personal computers. Since Visicalc would only run on Apple computers, the Apple Corporation went from two men in the garage to a major American Corporation in a very short time. Nowadays you can run a spreadsheet on any PC. You have a wide choice of computerised spreadsheet programs available including Lotus, Supercalc, Excel etc.

What is a Spreadsheet Package?

A spreadsheet is an arrangement of rows and columns to form a grid (see example on page 83). The columns run from left to right across the spreadsheet and are usually labelled with a letter starting at A, running through to Z, then AA, AB, AC etc. Most spreadsheets have at least 256 columns which takes you up to Column HP. Rows run from top to bottom down the spreadsheet and are numbered sequentially (1, 2, 3 etc), often going to 16,000 rows or even beyond.

Where a row and a column intersect, they form a 'cell'. Each cell can be referenced by the co-ordinates of its column letter and row number. For example, a spreadsheet going to column HP and row 8,192 would have 2,097,152 cells in the spreadsheet.

Data can be entered into the spreadsheet in the form of text, numbers and formulae. Formulae can consist of:

- numbers
- mathematical operations (eg add, subtract, multiply, divide etc)
- cell references.

Thus the formula '1+1' may be input giving the answer '2'. Or, you can tell the spreadsheet to add the contents of cell 'A1' to the contents of cell 'A2' and to put the result in cell 'A3'. A comprehensive range of mathematical, statistical and logical functions are available, if required.

A spreadsheet package is powerful because it can manipulate data. It is possible to:

• copy and move cells and blocks of cells within the spreadsheet
• insert or delete rows and columns
• erase the contents of cells
• carry out 'what if' analysis by substituting different values
• sort and rearrange data
• print out the result as hard copy or save it as a file for later retrieval
• build in links between different spreadsheets.

Hardcastle's Cashbook created in Excel

HARDCASTLES HARDWARE

	Date	Detail	Total	VAT	Sales	Other		Date	Detail	To Bank	Bank Payments	VAT	Materials	Travel & Petrol	Telephone	Light & Heat	Printing & Stationary	Wages	Sundries	Bankings
	INCOME							EXPENDITURE									January 199x			
	Bal B/Fwd	50.00						Bank Bal B/F												500.25
1-Jan	Sale	223.65	33.31	190.34			1-Jan	J Brown (stock)		423.46	63.07	360.39							
1-Jan	Sale	235.00	35.00	200.00			2-Jan	Banking	458.65										458.65
2-Jan	Sale	354.74	52.83	301.91			6-Jan	Banking	354.74										354.74
6-Jan	Sale	124.32	18.52	105.80			6-Jan	Wages		124.65							124.65		
6-Jan	Capital Introduced	1,000.00			1,000.00		10-Jan	B Telecom		84.56	12.59			71.97					
10-Jan	Sale	294.89	43.92	250.97			10-Jan	F Robinson (stock)		224.47	33.43	191.04							
12-Jan	Sale	264.33	39.37	224.96			12-Jan	Banking	1,124.32										1,124.32
15-Jan	Sale	324.78	48.37	276.41			10-Jan	Banking	294.89										294.89
15-Jan	Sale	110.66	16.48	94.18			15-Jan	Banking	264.33										264.33
18-Jan	Sale	142.56	21.23	121.33			15-Jan	Banking	435.44										435.44
19-Jan	Sale	210.45	31.34	179.11			18-Jan	Electricity		154.58	23.02				131.56				
21-Jan	Sale	189.46	28.22	161.24			18-Jan	Banking	142.56										142.56
21-Jan	Sale	88.44	13.17	75.27			19-Jan	Bank charges		20.00								20.00	
25-Jan	Sale	110.69	16.49	94.20			19-Jan	Banking	210.45										210.45
27-Jan	Sale	224.52	33.44	191.08			25-Jan	F Jones (stock)		445.98	66.42	379.56							
30-Jan	Sale	145.96	21.74	124.22			25-Jan	Banking	277.90										277.90
							27-Jan	Rates		564.12								564.12	
							27-Jan	Banking	110.69										110.69
							29-Jan	Bluett (stock)		324.58	48.34	276.24							
							29-Jan	Banking	224.52										224.52
							30-Jan	Banking	145.96										145.96
							30-Jan	Petty Cash		108.75	14.09		59.58			20.98		14.10	
	Column Totals	4,044.45	453.43	2,591.02	1,000.00				4,044.45	2,475.15	260.97	1,207.23	59.58	71.97	131.56	20.98	124.65	598.22	4,044.45

If you have a spreadsheet package, you can use it to computerise your manual cashbook. This will save a lot of tedious arithmetic and produce an output which will probably be neater than you can achieve by handwriting the text.

Programming your cashbook into a computer is a practical proposition for anyone who is familiar with spreadsheets. However, before you rush off and convert your manual cashbook to a computerised version, read the next part of this chapter. The idea of computerised book-keeping has been around for some while. Software houses have taken the basic idea much further than the spreadsheet, they have added a great deal of sophistication. This alternative approach may be better for you in the long run.

Computerised Book-keeping

Nowadays, most small businesses have a personal computer (PC) which they use for word processing. Inevitably, businessmen wonder whether they should use the computer to keep their books and accounts. For readers who fall into this category, here is a short guide to computerised accounting. If you want to know more, you should read *Accounting with Computers* which is another book in this series, devoted entirely to computerised accounting.

Attached to the back inside cover of this book, you will find a trial copy of Sage *Instant Accounting*. If you have access to a PC, why not install *Instant Accounting* and experiment with it as you read this chapter? If you like what you see, you can call Sage who will tell you how to convert your trial copy into a full copy at a discounted price.

How to Install Instant Accounting on Windows 95

- Insert your 'Instant' CD into your CD-ROM drive.

- Open the 'Start' menu and choose the 'Run' option. The Run dialogue box appears.

- In the 'Open' box, type **D:\setup** then choose the OK button. (If you are installing from a different drive, replace D: in the above command with the appropriate drive letter.)

- Follow the on-screen instructions to complete the installation.

How to Install Instant Accounting on Windows 3.11

- Insert your 'Instant' CD into your CD-ROM drive.

- Open the 'File' menu from the Program Manager menu bar and choose the 'Run' option. The Run dialogue box appears.

- In the Command Line text box, type **D:\setup** then choose the OK button. (If you are installing from a different drive, replace D: in the above command with the appropriate drive letter.)

- Follow the on-screen instructions to complete the installation.

We recommend that you accept the default values offered by the program during installation. Once the program is installed, you will be presented with the following screen.

We suggest that you run the *Instant Accounting Tour* by double clicking the Instant Tour icon.

When you have completed the tour, you can load the *Instant Accounting* program either by:

- double clicking the desktop icon, Instant Accounting   or

- from the Start menu by selecting 'Start' followed by 'Programs' followed by 'Instant Accounting 98' as follows.

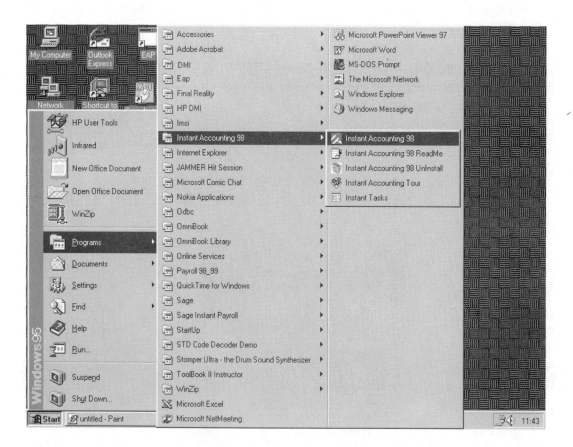

After a short while, the program will load and you will be presented with the following screen.

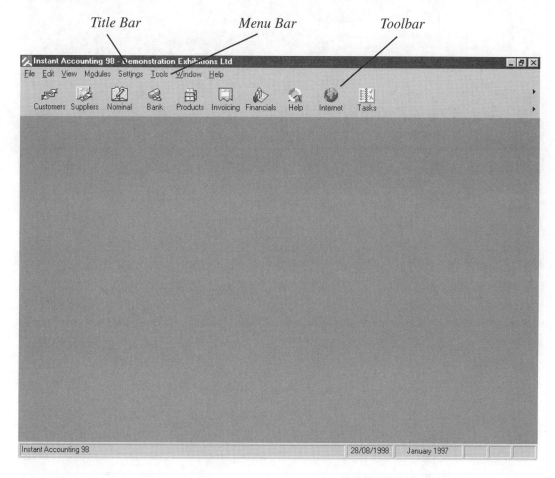

At the top of the screen, you can see three horizontal bands of information.These are:

Title Bar – the top line gives the program name (ie *Instant Accounting 98)* and the name of the business, eg Demonstration Exhibitions Ltd.

Menu Bar – the next line of information is called the menu bar. This contains menus for File, Edit, View, Modules, Settings etc. We recommend that you use the menu bar to load demonstration data for Demonstration Exhibitions Ltd as follows. Click on 'File', this will bring up the following menu.

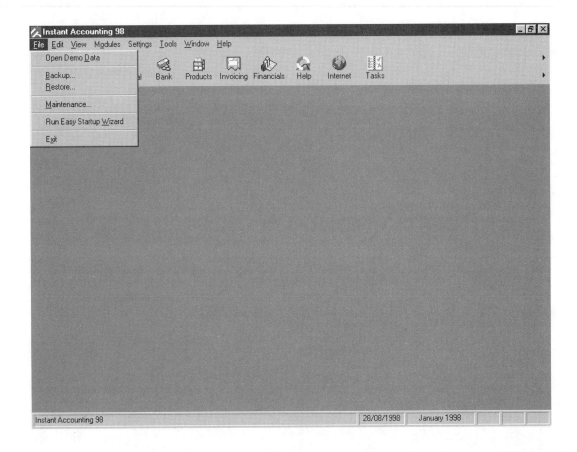

The top option in the menu box will be either 'Open Instant Data' or 'Open Demo Data'. Click the top option (if necessary) to make it read 'Open Demo Data'.

Toolbar – Below the menu bar is the toolbar. The toolbar contains a series of small pictures in boxes. These pictures are more properly called icons. Each icon has a word below it describing the purpose of that icon. We will shortly use the icons to navigate around the program.

This is what each icon does.

The 'Customers' option enables you to set up customer accounts, raise invoices, issue statements and control debt using aged debt reports. This ledger is particularly valuable to businesses operating credit sales.

The 'Suppliers' option enables you to set up supplier accounts and record invoices billed to you. It also enables you to check how much business you are doing with each supplier and manage your cash outflows for supplier payments.

The 'Nominal' option is used to record amounts of money passing through the accounts. It records receipts from sales, loans in and overdraft etc. It records expenditure on items like wages, expenses, capital equipment, stock, subcontractor payments etc.

This option records money movements. Money can be channelled through three avenues. These are banks, cash and credit cards. You can, of course, transfer money between accounts. You can use this option to reconcile the bank account with your own accounting records.

This option is particularly useful to businesses which sell goods. Each type of product is given a product code, product description, selling price, VAT code and unit of sale. Storing product details in this way saves a huge amount of time. When you raise invoices, you only have to call up the product code and all of the detail is entered onto the invoice automatically without the need for further typing.

Raising sales invoices can take a lot of time. It is easy to make mistakes on invoices with items like the price, discount, delivery address, VAT rate etc. The invoicing option simplifies raising of invoices and delivers a level of neatness which is difficult to match by manual typing. Invoices raised by the system can be posted automatically to the accounts. This means that your records are always up to date, leaving you in complete control of the sales side of the business.

This option helps you to control your finances. You can access an audit trail, trial balance, profit and loss account, balance sheet, budget and VAT account.

On line help is available in two ways. One source works in the same way as *Windows 95*. You can dial up help topics by subject or key words to invoke a short paragraph of helpful information. The second source of help is Sage's 'instant help' – this is a small window which remains on screen. It displays context sensitive help as you proceed through the program.

Many companies maintain websites which contain information useful to their customers. Sage is no exception. You can access the Sage website via the toolbar provided that you have a modem attached to the computer and a contract with an internet service provider like CompuServe, AOL etc.

The final option on the toolbar is the Tasks option. This is the electronic equivalent of a paper 'to do' list. You can remind yourself of the jobs that you should have done yesterday but didn't quite get round to!

A Look at the Ledgers

We haven't space in this book to look at the whole of the *Instant Accounting* program. For this, you need *Accounting with Computers*. However, we can take a quick look at three of the principal ledgers. By the way, don't be intimidated by the word 'ledgers'. In the old days, all accounts were maintained in big books called ledgers. Nowadays, of course, computerised accounts don't use ledgers. However, the term has stuck so many accountants still talk about ledgers even though the records are now stored electronically on a computer.

The Customer Module

Many packages call this the Sales Ledger, this is the traditional name for the part of the accounting system dealing with sales administration. Nowadays, the term 'sales ledger' sounds a bit formal and archaic so Sage has labelled this part of the system the 'Customers' menu which sounds more user-friendly.

The 'Customers' part of the program will be of particular value to businesses which offer credit to their customers. Selling goods or services on credit involves a huge amount of administration. You have to maintain records of cutomers' names, addresses and credit balances. You have to chase debt with statements, letters and telephone calls.

The next chapter shows you how to do this manually using a Sales Day Book and Sales Ledger Cards. However, manual methods are really only viable if you have a very small number of credit customers to look after. Computerised sales records of the kind shown here are immeasurably more efficient.

If you click the Customers icon in the main menu, you will be presented with the screen shown below.

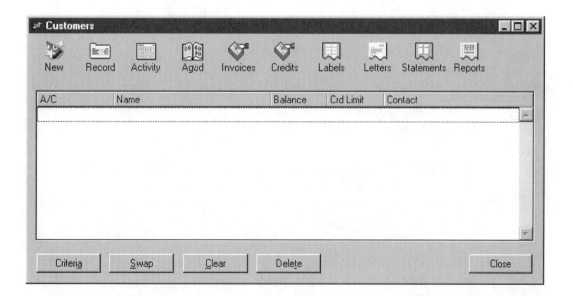

Each of the subsidiary icons has a function as follows.

This Wizard helps you set up a new customer account.

This option enables you to keep comprehensive records about your customers.

This option enables you to track sales activity for individual customers.

This option enables you to print out an aged debt report for each customer.

This option enables you to enter invoices raised manually. Most people won't use this option. They will use the Invoices option on the main menu which enables you to generate an invoice within the program.

This option enables you to enter credit notes onto the system which have previously been produced manually. Most people will not use this option, they will use the Credit Notes option within Invoicing on the main menu.

This option produces address labels which are useful if you want to send sales literature to your customers.

This option is particularly useful if you write to customers telling them that they have overdue accounts. The software 'personalises' the stationery by automatically inserting the appropriate name, address and amount owed.

Most businesses send their customers a statement of account every month. Statements remind customers that they owe money. Producing statements by hand is a nightmare. Generating statements on computers is a major benefit.

Instant Accounting comes preprogrammed with a range of useful sales management reports. These include reports like Top Customer List, customers over credit limit, customers' address list etc.

The Suppliers Ledger

Sage Instant Accounting calls this part of the software the 'Suppliers' module which sounds much more friendly than 'Purchase Ledger' which is the term generally used.

If you select the Supplier ledger from the main menu, you are presented with the following screen.

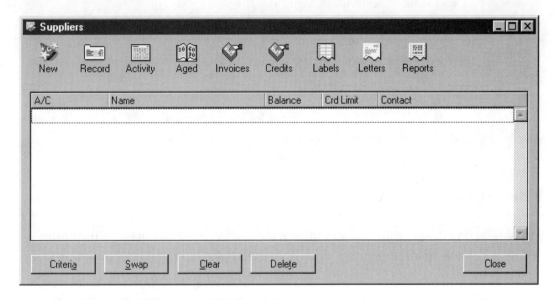

This is what the options within the Suppliers screen do.

Guides you through the set up for a new account.

Enables you to keep detailed records about suppliers including business name, address, contact name, terms of trade, history of transactions etc.

This option records the purchase history for that particular supplier.

Produces a report on how many days suppliers have been waiting for payment.

Enables you to enter a batch of purchase invoices into the computer.

 Enables you to input suppliers' credit notes into the computer.

 Enables you to produce name and address labels for your suppliers. Useful if you want to send them a circular.

 Enables you to send them a 'form letter'. This is a standard letter which has been 'customised' by the addition of their name and address.

 Instant Accounting includes a range of preprogrammed reports which most businesses will find useful. Examples include supplier address list, supplier activity, aged creditor analysis etc.

The Nominal Ledger

The Nominal Ledger records the amounts of money received and spent by the business during the course of an accounting year. If you select the Nominal Ledger option from the main menu, you will be presented with the following screen

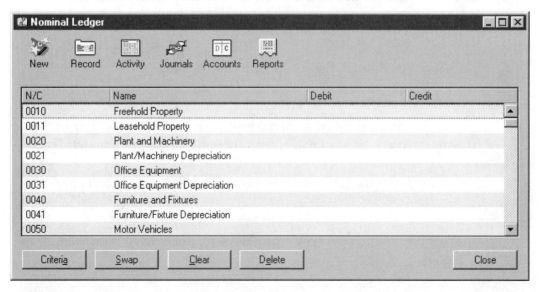

Notice that the window displays the types of income and expenditure recorded by Demonstration Exhibitions Ltd. If you scroll down the list, you will see the full range of account codes. Income and expenditure is coded because computers process numbers more effectively than text. Here is a list of the account codes used in the program.

Account Code Range

Fixed Assets	0000 – 999
Current Assets	1000 – 1999
Current Liabilities	2000 – 2999
Capital and Reserves	3000 – 3999
Sales	4000 – 4999
Purchases	5000 – 5999
Direct Expenses	6000 – 6999
Overheads	7000 – 7999

The Sub Menus

This is what the Nominal Ledger options do.

The Wizard guides you through the setting up of a new nominal ledger account.

This option is useful if you want to set up budgets. You can record last year's actual figure and this year's planned figure for each type of income and expenditure. This year's 'actual results' are added as the year proceeds.

This option enables you to select an item of income or expenditure and display the account history so far this year.

Sage operates under double entry book-keeping rules. This means that, if you choose the 'Journals' method of amending entries, you have to modify each account with debit and credit entries.

If you select the Accounts icon followed by 'Edit', you will be able to see the account categories. If you select an overhead category, eg purchases in the left hand description column, you will be able to see a breakdown of that category on the right hand side of the screen.

The software arrives with built-in nominal ledger reports. These include reports covering nominal balances, nominal list, day books etc.

Instant Accounting represents an ideal entry point for a business thinking of computerising its accounts. As the business grows, you can upgrade the software to include additional accounting functions like job costing, sales order processing, purchase order processing, fixed asset management etc.

Chapter 6

Book-keeping for Traders on 'Tax Point Accounting'

This chapter introduces two new aspects of book-keeping. These are:

- tax point accounting for VAT
- controlling credit.

Although the following pages show you how to handle these tasks manually, you should be aware that both of these procedures are time consuming and complicated to do by hand. *This is the point at which most businesses switch to computerised accounting.* Computerised accounting has many benefits including:

- a saving of time and effort
- accounting software is very reliable
- hardware and software is now cheap
- you can get better management reports from a computerised system.

However, for the technophobic and those who aren't yet ready for the transition to computerised accounts, here is an explanation of manual book-keeping for traders registered for VAT under tax point accounting. We start with an explanation of tax point accounting for VAT.

Tax Point Accounting for VAT

If your sales turnover exceeds the cash accounting limit, you are not allowed to use the cash accounting method. You have to base your VAT liability on something called the 'tax point'. You may remember that, under cash accounting, your VAT liability was based on the date that you received or paid out money. Under tax point accounting, your VAT liability is based on the dates on which invoices are *raised* not the dates on which they are *paid.*

We have just said that your VAT liability is based on the dates that invoices are raised. In fact, matters are slightly more complicated than this. Strictly speaking, your VAT liability is based on the 'tax point' date on the invoice, which can be slightly different from the date the invoice was raised.

Have a look at a few invoices. Notice that many of them simply bear an invoice date. However, some will show both an invoice date and a tax point date. Sometimes the tax point date is the same as the invoice date, sometimes it is different. How are we to make sense of all these dates?

Let's begin by explaining that Customs and Excise don't automatically accept your invoice date as the date of the transaction for VAT purposes. HM Customs and Excise have created an artificial transaction date called the tax point. This is important for tax point accounting because you account for VAT by collecting together all invoices bearing a tax point date falling within your VAT quarter.

How do you know what tax point to enter when you raise a sales invoice? Here are the rules in simplified form (for the full story, you need to read the VAT guide Notice 700).

- If you raise an invoice on the same date as the supply of the goods or services, the tax point date is the same as the invoice date.

- If you supply goods or services and issue an invoice within 14 days, the tax point date is again the same as the invoice date.

- If you supply goods or services and issue a tax invoice *more than 14 days after the supply,* the tax point is the date of supply of the goods or services.

- If you invoice your customers (or receive payment) *before* you supply the goods or service, the date of invoice (or payment) becomes the tax point.

If you receive *purchase* invoices which only show an invoice date, assume that the invoice date is the same as the tax point date.

We need to account for VAT based on the tax point date. This means that we have to find a system of recording sales and purchase invoices that will enable us to collect together invoices with a tax point date falling within our VAT quarter. This is usually done with a 'day book'.

A day book is simply a list of all sales, or purchase, invoices shown in date sequence. A sales day book example is shown on page 102. Most people would naturally choose invoice date as the logical sequence. However, if we are using the day book mainly to calculate VAT, you may prefer to list your invoices in tax point sequence since this would make completing the VAT return easier. You may even elect to record both invoice date and tax point date in adjacent columns where these differ, the choice is yours.

We will have a closer look at day books shortly. For the moment, however, we need to focus on the other new aspect introduced in this chapter which is credit control.

Controlling Credit

Very few businesses make all their transactions in cash.

- Most businesses receive credit from their suppliers.
- Most businesses offer credit to their trade customers.

You need some credit control system to ensure that:

- you pay your suppliers on time
- you get paid on time.

If you only have a few invoices, you can keep them in an 'unpaid invoices' file. Following payment, the invoice can be transferred to a 'paid invoices' file. Periodic trawls through the unpaid invoices file may be all that's needed to keep credit control up to date.

On the other hand, some businesses have too many invoices to handle in this way. They need to summarise the invoices so that they can see, at a glance, how much is owed to them, and how much they owe others. This can be achieved using day books. As invoices are received from suppliers, they are summarised in the Purchases Day Book. As invoices are sent to customers, they are summarised in the Sales Day Book. When an invoice is paid, an entry is made in the relevant day book so that the business can keep track of invoices both in and out. Notes on sales and purchases day books follow.

The Sales Day Book

The sales day book serves two main functions, these are:

- to calculate the output tax for your VAT return
- to control your debtors (ie people who owe you money).

An example of a sales day book is shown on page 102. Here is an explanation of the columns.

Column 1	Shows the invoice date (or tax point date) on the invoice.
Column 2	Shows your customer's name.
Column 3	Shows the invoice number. This should be consecutive as Customs and Excise look for this. If you spoil a numbered invoice, keep it – don't destroy it!
Column 4	Shows the total (or gross) amount of the invoice.
Column 5	Shows the VAT element of the invoice.
Columns 6 and 7	Show the net amount (ie excluding VAT). These columns can be used for analysing sales. In our case, we have analysed them into cash sales and credit sales. Of course, you may wish to analyse sales differently for your business. You could use sales by area, product type, kind of service, type of customer, salesperson etc.
Column 8	This column is used for credit control. Enter the date when customers pay off their debt. This way you can see at a glance who still owes you money. We don't need to record the date paid for 'cash sales' since the customer pays when he collects the goods.

Sales Day Book – Example

1 Date	2 Customer	3 Inv No	4 Gross Amount	5 VAT	6 Cash Sales	7 Credit Sales	8 Date Paid	9 Remarks
1/1/199x	M O'Brian	76	153.26	22.83	130.43		—	
7/1/199x	J Smith	77	47.35	7.05		40.30	17/1/199x	
10/1/199x	Cash Sales		45.00	6.70	38.30		—	
12/1/199x	B Jones	78	117.50	17.50	100.00		—	
14/1/199x	S Green	79	235.00	35.00		200.00	20/2/199x	
15/1/199x	Cash Sales		51.00	7.60	43.40		—	
17/1/199x	P Blue	80	58.75	8.75	50.00		—	
19/1/199x	J Smith	81	352.50	52.50	300.00		—	
20/1/199x	M Jacks Ltd	82	1235.00	183.94		1051.06	29/2/199x	
Totals			2295.36	341.87	662.13	1291.36		

Exercise 12

Why not have a go at constructing a sales day book for yourself using the following data and the blank pro forma on page 104.

Date	Customer	Inv	Gross	VAT	Cash	Credit	Date Paid	Remarks
March 1	J Smith	121	235.00	35.00		200.00	1/4/9x	
1	Cash Sales		564.05	84.01	480.04			
2	W Smith	122	381.87	56.87		325.00	10/4/9x	
2	Cash Sales		425.97	63.44	362.53			
3	S Robins	123	440.63	65.63		375.00	15/4/9x	
3	Cash Sales		294.58	43.87	250.71			
4	D Rees	124	235.00	35.00		200.00		
4	Cash Sales		356.98	53.17	303.81			
5	D Power	125	117.50	17.50		100.00	21/3/9x	
5	Cash Sales		521.45	77.66	443.79			

Add all the columns up and check your answers with those on page 166.

Sales Day Book

Date	Customer	Inv No	Gross Amount	VAT	Cash Sales (net)	Credit Sales (net)	Date Paid	Remarks
Totals								

The Purchase Day Book

The purchase day book serves two main functions. These are:

- to calculate your input tax for the VAT return
- to control your business creditors (people who you owe money to).

The purchase day book operates in a similar way to the sales day book. Look at the example on page 106. Here is an explanation of the columns.

Column 1 – is the tax point or invoice date on the invoice that you have received. You should choose which date you want to record. Exceptionally, you may decide to list both. But remember that the tax point is the most important date for VAT purposes.

Column 2 – is the name of your supplier.

Column 3 – is your own reference number. If you enter this number on the invoice prominently, it will save time when you have to find an old invoice.

Column 4 – is for entering the total (or gross) amount of the invoice.

Column 5 – is for entering the VAT relating to that invoice.

Column 6 – is for entering the net amount of the invoice.

Column 7 – is for entering the date you pay the invoice.

Further columns can be added for an analysis of expenditure, if required, but be careful that you are not simply duplicating the analysis in your analysed cashbook. If most of your transactions are based on cash, you will probably find the analysed cashbook the best place to analyse your expenditure. On the other hand, if most of your transactions are based on credit (and particularly if you are accounting for VAT based on the tax point date), you will probably find the day book the best place for your analysis. Why don't you have a go at the purchase day book exercise on page 107?

Purchase Day Book – Example

1 Date	2 Supplier	3 Ref No	4 Gross Amt	5 VAT	6 Net Amt	7 Date Paid	8 Stock (net)	9 Motor (net)	10 Tel (net)	11 Stat (net)	12 Other (net)
1/1/199x	J Smith	126	115.00	17.13	97.87	3/1/9x	97.87				
2/1/199x	Petrol	127	20.00	2.98	17.02	2/1/9x		17.02			
7/1/199x	J Jones	129	600.00	89.36	510.64	15/1/9x	510.64				
7/1/199x	Brit Telecom	130	46.00	6.85	39.15	17/1/9x			39.15		
8/1/199x	Stock	131	296.00	44.09	251.91	18/1/9x	251.91				
19/1/199x	Taxi	132	4.60	.69	3.91	19/1/9x		3.91			
19/1/199x	J Smith	133	345.00	51.38	293.62	15/4/9x	293.62				
19/1/199x	Berts	134	460.00	68.51	391.49	3/3/9x	391.49				
Totals			1886.60	280.99	1605.61		1545.53	20.93	39.15		

Exercise 13

Enter the following purchases on the blank purchase day book on page 108.

Date	Supplier	Ref No	Gross Amount	VAT	Net Amount	Date Paid
			£	£	£	
1/3/9x	D Roberts (Stock)	101	117.50	17.50	100.00	25/4/9x
1/3/9x	Petrol	102	20.00	2.98	17.02	01/3/9x
1/3/9x	Print Co (Stationery)	103	58.75	8.75	50.00	
2/3/9x	T Brown (Stock)	104	256.98	38.27	218.71	31/3/9x
2/3/9x	Telephone	105	98.86	14.72	84.14	31/3/9x
2/3/9x	Petrol	106	25.00	3.72	21.28	02/3/9x
3/3/9x	J Jones (Stock)	107	545.62	81.26	464.36	15/4/9x
3/3/9x	Repairs	108	62.23	9.27	52.96	03/3/9x
4/3/9x	D S Ben (Stock)	109	22.36	3.33	19.03	04/3/9x
5/3/9x	Postage*	110	10.00	0.00	10.00	05/3/9x
5/3/9x	Garage (Motor exps)	111	58.46	8.71	49.75	05/3/9x

* We have entered postage in the purchase day book even though it is exempt from VAT. This is because we need to include all purchase inputs in box 7 of the VAT return including those which are exempt and zero rated.

Check your answers against the model shown on page 167.

Purchase Day Book – Example

1 Date	2 Supplier	3 Ref No	4 Gross Amt	5 VAT	6 Net Amt	7 Date Paid	8 Stock (net)	9 Motor (net)	10 Tel (net)	11 Stat (net)	12 Other (net)
Totals											

Cashbooks for Tax Point Traders

Cashbooks for tax point traders look the same as those used by cash accounting traders.

You still need to record 'VAT in' and 'VAT out', as before, because you have to extract the VAT from your transactions.

We could show exactly the same layout as we used for Hardcastle's cash accounting books. However, to add extra value to this section and to illustrate that cashbooks are very flexible, we have chosen to introduce a couple of minor changes in layout that demonstrate the flexibility of cashbook accounting. Have a look at the cashbook layout on page 116. There are two differences from the Hardcastle books used in Chapter 4.

Sonny Sunblinds gives its customers credit and Sonny has decided that he would like to record 'cash receipts' and 'credit receipts' separately, using a column for each. The 'credit receipts' column records cash received now for payment of invoices which could, of course, have been raised many weeks before.

The second difference concerns column 10 on page 116. Have a look at the page. Notice that column 10 is labelled 'Bankings/Cash Out'. This column is a little bit more complicated than the system we recorded for Hardcastle but it does allow you to record cash payments from the 'till' if this flexibility is required. The logic works as follows. Money collected by the business can either be spent as cash or deposited at the bank – there are no other destinations available. This means that column 10 traps *all* money going out of the business, whether spent as cash or banked. Money which is banked *also* has an entry in column 20, ie bankings. Expenditures which do not have an entry in column 20 must be cash expenditures on this method of working.

Now let's see how to keep the analysed cashbook under tax point accounting. The best way to illustrate the method is by way of example. We will use Sonny Sunblinds. Remember that, although we will be extracting VAT throughout this exercise, we cannot use the VAT figures in the cashbook directly to compile our VAT return. The VAT is being extracted in the cashbook purely to derive the net of VAT figures which are used to produce the accounts.

Sonny Sunblinds Example

Sonny runs a manufacturing business making a variety of sunblinds for both interior and exterior use. Sonny supplies the blinds to retail outlets on cash or credit terms from his factory. His completed analysed cashbook for the month of January is shown on page 116. Let's see how this was built up. To start with, we will look at the left hand side which records 'income'.

Recording Income

Here is a record of Sonny's income for January.

Date		Transaction	Receipts from Cash Sales (incl VAT)	Receipts from Credit Sales (incl VAT)	Other Income (not VATable)
			£	£	£
Jan	1	Cash sale	2350.00		
	1	Cash sale	1762.50		
	8	Credit sale		2937.50	
	9	Cash sale	940.00		
	10	Capital introduced			3000.00
	14	Cash sale	5875.00		
	15	Credit sale		4700.00	
	16	Cash sale	2350.00		
	19	Cash sale	8518.75		
	22	Credit sale		6462.50	
	24	Cash sale	7343.75		
	26	Cash sale	587.50		
	28	Cash sale	14687.50		
	31	Cash sale	587.50		
		Total	**45002.50**	**14100.00**	**3000.00**

Notice in the table below that Sonny has recorded cash sales, credit sales and other income separately. 'Other income' comprises everything except 'sales' (eg a bank loan, interest received on bank deposits, or sale of assets). Notice also that capital introduced is not VATable. All the sales figures include VAT. We need to extract the VAT as we enter these figures into our books. The entries in the credit sales column are cash receipts from sales previously made on credit. The date alongside the credit sales entry is the date on which payment is received. The sale itself could, of course, have been made many weeks before.

We have already said that we believe it is good accounting practice to bank all money received intact. Although we recommend this discipline, we know that, in practice, some businesses will still insist on paying out cash from the till. The method used in this section enables the book-keeper to cater for this eventuality should it happen.

Recording income!

The entries are recorded below. VAT has been extracted from the gross receipts using the VAT fraction calculated in Chapter 2. You may remember that the VAT fraction for the 17½% rate of VAT is 7/47.

Income

1 Date	2 Detail	3 Total		4 VAT		5 Cash		6 Credit		7 Other		
Jan 1	Cash Sale	2350	00	350	00	2000	00					
1	Cash Sale	1762	50	262	50	1500	00					
8	Credit Sale	2937	50	437	50			2500	00			
9	Cash Sale	940	00	140	00	800	00					
10	Capital Introduced	3000	00							3000	00	
14	Cash Sale	5875	00	875	00	5000	00					
15	Credit Sale	4700	00	700	00			4000	00			
16	Cash Sale	2350	00	350	00	2000	00					
19	Cash Sale	8518	75	1268	75	7250	00					
22	Credit Sale	6462	50	962	50			5500	00			
24	Cash Sale	7343	75	1093	75	6250	00					
26	Cash Sale	587	50	87	50	500	00					
28	Cash Sale	14687	50	2187	50	12500	00					
31	Cash Sale	587	50	87	50	500	00					
	Totals	62102	50	8802	50	38300	00	12000	00	3000	00	

Recording Expenditure

During the month of January, Sonny also suffered a range of expenses. These were as follows:

Date	Transaction	Amount (incl VAT) £	Comment
Jan 1	Jay's Fabrics (materials)	2608.50	Paid by cheque
1	Car service	305.50	Paid by cheque
2	Petrol	30.00	Paid by cash
3	Banking	4112.50	
4	Stationery	535.80	Paid by cheque
7	Wages	2896.00	Direct charge
8	Banking	2937.50	
11	Banking	3940.00	
12	Die Cast Ltd (materials)	17037.50	Paid by cheque
14	Banking	5875.00	
15	British Telecom	638.02	Paid by cheque
15	Petrol	30.00	Paid by cash
15	Entertainment	52.87	Paid by cash *
15	Banking	4700.00	
18	Electricity	941.55	Paid by chq - VAT at 17½% non domestic
19	Banking	10868.75	
21	Jay's Fabrics (materials)	6403.75	Paid by cheque
21	Petrol	35.00	Paid by cash
22	Rates	869.00	Paid by cheque
23	Advertising	528.75	Paid by cheque
23	Banking	6462.50	
25	Office supplies	493.50	Paid by cheque
25	Banking	7343.75	
26	Office sundries	16.20	Paid by cash
26	Banking	587.50	
26	Petrol	30.00	Paid by cash
27	Petty cash	129.40	Paid by cheque
28	Die Cast Ltd (materials)	6580.00	Paid by cheque
29	Banking	14687.50	
29	Road fund licence	135.00	Paid by cheque
31	Banking	587.50	

* **Note:** VAT cannot be reclaimed on entertainment

We will now break this expenditure down into columns. Each column collects together similar kinds of expenditure. We will record:

- how much cash we spent in total
- whether payment was made by cash or cheque
- where the money has gone to, eg wages, travel, materials, bank etc
- how much VAT was included in the expenditure, if any.

We show below how we would record these expenditures. Why not tick back the payments on page 116 against the entries below checking that you agree each one as you go?

Recording payments

Expenditure

8	9	10	11	12	13	14	15	16	17	18	19	20
Date	Detail	Bankings/ Cash Out	Bank Payments	VAT	Materials	Travel + Petrol	Tele- phone	Light + Heat	Printing Staty	Wages	Sundries	Bankings
Jan 1	Jay's Fabrics		2608 50	388 50	2220 00							
1	Car Service		305 50	45 50		260 00						
2	Petrol	30 00		4 47		25 53						
3	Banking	4112 50										4112 50
4	Stationery		535 80	79 80					456 00			
7	Wages		2896 00							2896 00		
8	Banking	2937 50										2937 50
11	Banking	3940 00										3940 00
12	Die Cast Ltd		17037 50	2537 50	14500 00							
14	Banking	5875 00										5875 00
15	British Telecom		638 02	95 02			543 00					
15	Petrol	30 00		4 47		25 53						
15	Entertainment	52 87									52 87	
15	Banking	4700 00										4700 00
18	Electricity		941 55	140 23				801 32				
19	Banking	10868 75										10868 75
21	Jay's Fabrics		6403 75	953 75	5450 00							
21	Petrol	35 00		5 21		29 79						
22	Rates		869 00								869 00	
23	Advertising		528 75	78 75							450 00	
23	Banking	6462 50										6462 50
25	Office Supplies		493 50	73 50					420 00			
25	Banking	7343 75										7343 75
26	Office Sundries	16 20									16 20	
26	Banking	587 50										587 50
26	Petrol	30 00		4 47		25 53						
27	Petty Cash		129 40								129 40	
28	Die Cast Ltd		6580 00	980 00	5600 00							
29	Banking	14687 50										14687 50
29	Road Fund Licence		135 00			135 00						
31	Banking	587 50										587 50
	Totals	62296 57	40102 27	5391 17	27770 00	501 38	543 00	801 32	876 00	2896 00	1517 47	62102 50

Cross Casting the Totals

We cross cast the totals to make sure that we have eliminated silly arithmetical errors. The cross cast totals have been entered on page 116.

Cross casting the totals

Cross Casting the Income Totals

Notice on page 116 how all the columns have been added up. They can then be cross cast. On the income side, the totals of columns 4 to 7 must add up to the total of column 3, viz:

	£	£
Total Income Column 3		**62102.50**
Column 4 VAT	8802.50	
Column 5 Cash Sales	38300.00	
Column 6 Credit Sales	12000.00	
Column 7 Other Income	3000.00	
Total Columns 4–7		**62102.50**

Everyone makes mistakes with their entries and additions. 'Cross casting' the totals helps eliminate these mistakes.

Cross Casting the Expenditure Totals

Notice on page 116 how the totals of columns 10 and 11 add up to the totals of columns 12–20, viz:

		£	£
Column 10	Bankings & Cash Out	62296.57	
Column 11	Bank Payments	40102.27	
Total Columns 10 and 11			**102398.84**
Column 12	VAT	5391.17	
Column 13	Materials	27770.00	
Column 14	Travel, petrol etc	501.38	
Column 15	Telephone	543.00	
Column 16	Light, heat	801.32	
Column 17	Printing, stationery	876.00	
Column 18	Wages	2896.00	
Column 19	Sundries	1517.47	
Column 20	Bankings	62102.50	
Total Columns 12–20			**102398.84**

Reconciling the Cash

The closing balance in your cashbook should agree with the amount of cash you physically have in hand. If the two don't agree then you have probably made one of the following mistakes.

- Someone has paid out cash without an entry appearing in the books.

- Someone has received cash without an entry appearing in the books.

- The entries in the cashbook have been copied down wrongly. This is why you cross cast your columns before cash reconciliation. It helps get the arithmetic correct. This should make cash reconciliation quicker.

- Giving and receiving the wrong change.

Sonny Sunblinds — January 19xx

Income

1 Date	2 Detail	3 Total	4 VAT	5 Cash Sales	6 Credit Sales	7 Other Income
Jan 1	Cash Sale	2350 00	350 00	2000 00		
1	Cash Sale	1762 50	262 50	1500 00		
8	Credit Sale	2937 50	437 50		2500 00	
9	Cash Sale	940 00	140 00	800 00		
10	Capital Introduced	3000 00				3000 00
14	Cash Sale	5875 00	875 00	5000 00		
15	Credit Sale	4700 00	700 00		4000 00	
16	Cash Sale	2350 00	350 00	2000 00		
19	Cash Sale	8518 75	1268 75	7250 00		
22	Credit Sale	6462 50	962 50		5500 00	
24	Cash Sale	7343 75	1093 75	6250 00		
26	Cash Sale	587 50	87 50	500 00		
28	Cash Sale	14687 50	2187 50	12500 00		
31	Cash Sale	587 50	87 50	500 00		
	Column Totals	62102 50	8802 50	38300 00	12000 00	3000 00

£62102.50

Expenditure

8 Date	9 Detail	10 Bankings/ Cash Out	11 Bank Payments	12 VAT	13 Materials	14 Travel + Petrol	15 Telephone	16 Light + Heat	17 Printing Stationery	18 Wages	19 Sundries	20 Bankings
Jan 1	Jay's Fabrics		2608 50	388 50	2220 00							
1	Car service		305 50	45 50		260 00						
2	Petrol	30 00		4 47		25 53						
3	Banking	4112 50										4112 50
4	Stationery		535 80	79 80					456 00			
7	Wages		2896 00							2896 00		
8	Banking	2937 50										2937 50
11	Banking	3940 00										3940 00
12	Die Cast Ltd		17037 50	2537 50	14500 00							
14	Banking	5875 00										5875 00
15	British Telecom		638 02	95 02			543 00					
15	Petrol	30 00		4 47		25 53						
15	Entertainment	52 87									52 87	
18	Banking	4700 00										4700 00
18	Electricity		941 55	140 23				801 32				
19	Banking	10868 75										10868 75
21	Jay's Fabrics		6403 75	953 75	5450 00							
21	Petrol	35 00		5 21		29 79						
22	Rates		869 00								869 00	
23	Advertising		528 75	78 75							450 00	
23	Banking	6462 50										6462 50
25	Office Supplies		493 50	73 50					420 00			
25	Banking	7343 75										7343 75
26	Office Sundries	16 20									16 20	
26	Banking	587 50										587 50
26	Petrol	30 00		4 47		25 53						
27	Petty Cash		129 40								129 40	
28	Die Cast Ltd		6580 00	980 00	5600 00							
29	Banking	14687 50										14687 50
29	Road fund licence		135 00			135 00						
31	Banking	587 50										587 50
	Column Totals	62296 57	40102 27	5391 17	27770 00	501 38	543 00	801 32	876 00	2896 00	1517 47	62102 50

£102398.84

£102398.84

116

If you don't find any mistakes or omissions to account for the discrepancy, it may be caused by theft.

You will see that the total 'income' received on page 116 (column 3) amounted to £62,102.50. The total 'bankings and cash out' figure (column 10) for the same period was £62,296.57. Assume the cash brought forward from the previous month was £250.

This means that on 31 January Sonny's cash balance should be:

		£	
	Opening Cash Balance b/fwd	250.00	
Add	Money in	62102.50	(column 3)
		62352.50	
Less	Money out	62296.57	(column 10)
	Closing Cash Balance c/fwd	55.93	

If Sonny's cash in hand does indeed amount to £55.93 then everything is fine. If, however, it does not equal £55.93, we need to do some detective work to find out why. For example:

- have all the entries in the cash book been entered correctly?

- was the opening balance figure brought forward from the previous month correctly?

- is the arithmetic correct?

- has anyone 'borrowed' any money?

- can anyone remember anything happening that may have caused the mistake?

Reconciling the cash

What if the worse comes to the worst and we can't agree the cash in hand with the books? We have no alternative but to adjust the carry forward figure to reflect the actual amount of cash in hand. This can be done with a 'mistakes' entry in the miscellaneous column. Too many mistakes are a symptom of carelessness on someone's part. Perhaps we should look at the way cash is handled to see if we need to make any changes to the cash handling system.

An Alternative Way of Recording Brought Forward Items

Please turn to page 124 now and note we have added a few more lines to the basic cashbook already shown on page 116. The cash balance brought forward (which was £250) has been entered towards the *bottom* of column 3 (previously we have shown it at the top of the page). The cash balance carried forward to February (which was £55.93) has also been recorded towards the *bottom* of column 10. You can obviously put the brought forward amounts at the top or bottom of each column; the arithmetic adds up correctly, whichever you choose. Here we are showing an alternative presentation to illustrate the variety of approaches used by book-keepers. We will use these figures later to 'balance the books'.

Reconciling the Bank Account

Reconciling the bank account ensures that you have the same amount of money shown on your bank statement as you have recorded in your cashbook. The bank is easier to balance because you have a bank statement to check your banking entries against. You will remember that differences can arise because:

- The bank account shows entries not in your cashbook, eg
  - bank charges
  - direct debits which you have forgotten to enter in your cash book
  - bank automated clearing service (BACS) payments into your account for which you have no notification
  - bank mispostings.

- Your cashbook shows entries not in your bank account. Normally these will be unpresented cheques or payments made into the bank too late in the day to appear on that day's bank statement.

- Mistaken entries by you, eg transposing numbers in the cashbook or simply copying wrong numbers into your cashbook. This is why you should cross cast your columns before doing a bank reconciliation. Cross casting takes out the silly arithmetical mistakes. This will save time when you reconcile the bank account.

Let's look at Sonny's bank statement for the period ended 31 January.

Date		Particulars	Payments £	Receipts £	Balance £
Jan	1	Opening Balance			18492.20
Jan	3	Jay's Fabrics	2608.50		15883.70
	3	Car service	305.50		15578.20
	3	Sundry credit		4112.50	19690.70
	7	Stationery	535.80		19154.90
	7	Wages	2896.00		19196.40
	8	Sundry credit		2937.50	22092.40
	11	Sundry credit		3940.00	23136.40
	14	Die Cast Ltd	17037.50		6098.90
	14	Sundry credit		5875.00	11973.90
	15	Sundry credit		4700.00	16673.90
	18	British Telecom	638.02		16035.88
	19	Sundry credit		10868.75	26904.63
	20	Electricity	941.55		25963.08
	23	Jay's Fabrics	6403.75		19559.33
	23	Sundry credit		6462.50	26021.83
	25	Rates	869.00		25152.83
	25	Sundry credit		7343.75	32496.58
	26	Advertising	528.75		31967.83
	26	Sundry credit		587.50	32555.33
	27	Petty cash	129.40		32425.93
	28	Office supplies	493.50		31932.43
		Closing Balance c/fwd			31932.43

Bank Statement – Sonny Sunblinds

We can now reconcile Sonny's bank balance with the cashbook. Notice that the balance shown on the bank statement is £31,932.43. The bank balance worked out from the cashbook is £40,492.43, calculated as follows:

		£	
	Opening Bank Bal b/fwd	18492.20	(balance b/fwd from Dec)
Add	Bankings	62102.50	(column 20)
		80594.70	
Less	Cheques	40102.27	(column 11)
	Closing Bank Bal c/fwd	40492.43	

For the purpose of this exercise, we have chosen to use the same opening balance (£18,492.20) for both the cashbook and the bank statement. In real life, this would rarely happen. You should always use the balance brought forward from the previous month's cashbook, not the bank statement.

How do we reconcile this difference? If you tick the cashbook entries back against the bank statement, you will find that there are four entries in the cashbook which do not appear on the bank statement. These are:

28 January	Die Cast Ltd	£6,580.00
29 January	Banking	£14,687.50
29 January	Road Fund Licence	£135.00
31 January	Banking	£587.50

If we include these entries which were in the cashbook but not on the bank statement, we have:

Reconciling the bank

Bank Reconciliation at 31 January

			£
Balance per bank statement at 31 January			31932.43
Add Bankings not recorded:			
	29 January	14687.50	
	31 January	587.50	
			15275.00
			47207.43
Less Unrepresented cheques for payment			
	28 January	6580.00	
	29 January	135.00	
			6715.00
Bank Balance per Cashbook c/fwd			40492.43

As a matter of interest, we may find that our *next* bank statement, ie that for February, would probably start as follows:

Bank Statement - Sonny Sunblinds

Date		Particulars	Payments £	Receipts £	Balance £
Feb	1	Opening Balance			31932.43
Feb	1	Sundry credit		14687.50	46619.93
	1	Sundry credit		587.50	47207.43
	1	Die Cast Ltd	6580.00		40627.43
	2	Road Fund Licence	135.00		40492.43

Notice that, at this point, the bank balance is the same as the figure in the cashbook. This is because the items missing from the previous bank statement have now had time to work their way through the banking system.

Please turn to page 124. You will see that we have shown the bank balance brought forward figure for December (which was £18,492.20) towards the bottom of column 20. We have also recorded the bank balance carried forward to February (which was £40,492.43) towards the foot of column 11. We will need these figures later when we 'balance the books'.

Balancing the Books

This is the final stage of book-keeping. It pulls together all the work undertaken so far. If your books balance, you can be pretty sure that you have eliminated all errors and omissions.

Please turn to page 124. Notice that there are four boxes labelled either 'Balancing the Cash' or 'Balancing the Bank'.

If both 'Balancing the Cash' boxes balance, you can be pretty sure that you have got your cash right. If both 'Balancing the Bank' boxes balance, you should have no trouble with your bank balance.

Balancing the Cash Totals

If you think about **cash** for the moment, the following relationship must hold true.

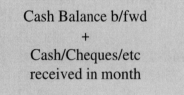

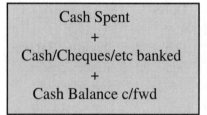

We can check these figures easily.

- Cash balance *brought forward* to this month is the cash balance *carried forward* from last month (you get this from last months' records).

- Cash/cheques/etc received for the month is the total of column 3.

- The sum of 'cash spent' and 'cash/cheques/etc banked' is the total of column 10.

- The cash balance carried forward is the cash balance you should have 'on hand'.

With any luck all of these figures should balance first time. Notice how we have inserted the cash balance brought forward in column 3 on page 124. This gives us a cash balance brought forward figure of £250 plus income for the month of £62,102.50, giving a balancing total of £62,352.50. It is no accident, of course, that this adds up to the total at the bottom of column 10, which is the sum of cash spent plus bankings plus cash balance carried forward. Our cashbooks, therefore, balance at £62,352.50.

Balancing the Bank Totals

The following relationships must hold good for our dealings with the bank.

Bank Balance b/fwd + Bankings in the month	*must equal*	Cheques etc written + Bank Balance c/fwd

We have inserted the appropriate figures in the boxes labelled 'Balancing the Bank'. In our case, the numbers balance so we have 'balanced the bank'.

We can check the figures as follows.

- Bank balance brought forward is the *reconciled* bank balance according to our cashbook at the end of last month. See that this has been entered as £18,492.20 towards the bottom of column 20 on page 124.

- 'Banking in the month' comprises £62,102.50 shown in column 20. Adding £18,492.20 bank balance brought forward to our month's bankings of £62,102.50 gives us a balancing total of £80,594.70.

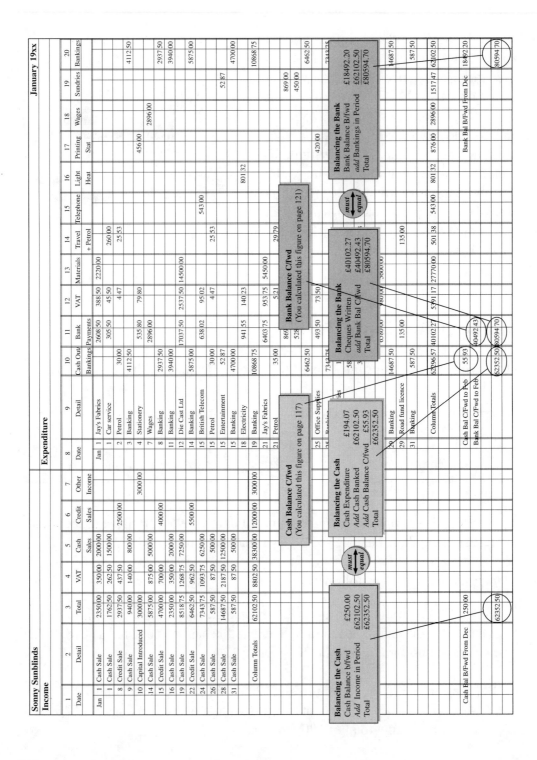

- The value of 'cheques etc written' is shown in column 11 on page 124 as £40,102.27. This column will comprise cheques written plus direct debits out etc.

- The bank balance carried forward will be the *reconciled* bank balance as per your cashbook. In our example this comes to £40,492.43 which is also entered in column 11 on page 124. Adding the two values together in column 11 gives our second balancing bank total which adds up to £80,594.70. Our bank totals, therefore, balance.

Completing the VAT Return

We now need to calculate the VAT owed to HMC&E. For the purpose of example, we will use the January entries on the sales and purchase day books on pages 102 and 106.

If you turn to the sales day book on page 102, you will see that the VAT due for January is £341.87. The VAT to offset against this from the purchase day book for January on page 106 is £280.99. This means that you would pay £60.88 for the month of January. Don't forget that the key dates on the sales and purchase day books are the tax point dates (not the invoice dates where they differ, or the payment dates). We are simply using the January figures as an example. Normally, of course, you would add up all the months within a VAT quarter. You don't usually do a return for a single month. We can now complete boxes 1 to 5 assuming we have no EC exports or imports (see page 126). However, we still need to work out the figures for boxes 6 and 7.

Under tax point accounting, the sales figure in box 6 on the VAT return is calculated by adding together the 'net sales' figures on all the invoices bearing a tax point date falling within our VAT quarter. In our case, the net sales figure on page 102 amounts to £662.13 + £1,291.36 which gives a total of £1,953.49. Note the difference here between cash accounting and tax point accounting. If you have previously used cash accounting, you will be used to entering the total amount of cash received during the VAT quarter. *This no longer applies.*

Value Added Tax Return

For the period

HM Customs and Excise

Your VAT Office telephone number is

For Official Use

Registration Number	Period

You could be liable to a financial penalty it your completed return and all the VAT payable are not received by the due date.

Due date:

For Official Use	

Before you fill in this form please read the notes on the back and the VAT leaflet *"Filling in your VAT return"*. Fill in all boxes clearly in ink, and write 'none' where necessary. Don't put a dash or leave any box blank. If there are no pence write "**00**" in the pence column. **Do not** enter more than one amount in any box.

For official use			£	p
	VAT due in this period on **sales** and other outputs	1	341	87
	VAT due in this period on **acquisitions** from other **EC Member States**	2	None	
	Total VAT due **(the sum of boxes 1 and 2)**	3	341	87
	VAT reclaimed in this period on **purchases** and other inputs (including acquisitions from the EC)	4	280	99
	Net VAT to be paid to Customs or reclaimed by you **(Difference between boxes 3 and 4)**	5	60	88
	Total value of **sales** and all other outputs excluding any VAT. **Include your box 8 figure**	6	1953	00
	Total value of **purchases** and all other inputs excluding any VAT. **Include your box 9 figure**	7	1605	00
	Total value of all **supplies** of goods and related services, excluding any VAT, to other **EC Member States**	8	None	00
	Total value of all **acquisitions** of goods and related services, excluding any VAT, from other **EC Member States**	9	None	00

Retail schemes. If you have used any of the schemes in the period covered by this return, enter the relevant letter(s) in this box.

If you are enclosing a payment please tick this box.

DECLARATION: You, or someone on your behalf, must sign below.

I,..declare that the
(Full name of signatory in BLOCK LETTERS)

information given above is true and complete.

Signature...Date.............19......

A false declaration can result in prosecution.

L

VAT 100

126

Under tax point accounting, the purchases figure in box 7 of the VAT return is calculated by adding together all the net purchase figures on invoices bearing a date which falls within our VAT quarter. In our case, the figure taken from page 106 is £1,605.61. We can, therefore, use the sales and purchase day books to calculate the:

- value of the VAT on outputs in box 1
- value of the VAT on inputs in box 4
- value of sales in box 6
- value of purchases in box 7.

A VAT return based on January's figure only is shown on page 126.

If you suffer bad debt on sales, have a look at Appendix 2 which tells you how to get bad debt relief on the VAT element of the sale.

If you are reclaiming motoring expenses, don't forget to include scale charges in boxes 1 and 6 (see page 67 for fuel scale charges example).

Exercise 14 – Completing the VAT Return

Use the sales and purchase day books from Exercises 12 and 13 to complete the following VAT return. Here's a reminder of the numbers that you need.

	£	
Output Tax	. . . .	(box 1)
Input Tax		(box 4)
Due to HMC&E		(box 5)
Sales Outputs		
Cash Sales	. . . .	
Credit Sales		
Total Sales Outputs		(box 6)
Purchase Inputs		(box 7)

Check your answer with pages 168 and 169.

Value Added Tax Return

For the period

HM Customs
and Excise

Exercise 14 (contd)

Your VAT Office telephone number is

For Official Use

Registration Number   Period

You could be liable to a financial penalty it your completed return and all the VAT payable are not received by the due date.

Due date:

For Official Use

Before you fill in this form please read the notes on the back and the VAT leaflet *"Filling in your VAT return"*. Fill in all boxes clearly in ink, and write 'none' where necessary. Don't put a dash or leave any box blank. If there are no pence write **"00"** in the pence column. **Do not** enter more than one amount in any box.

£   p

For official use		1	
	VAT due in this period on **sales** and other outputs	**1**	
	VAT due in this period on **acquisitions** from other **EC Member States**	**2**	
	Total VAT due **(the sum of boxes 1 and 2)**	**3**	
	VAT reclaimed in this period on **purchases** and other inputs (including acquisitions from the EC)	**4**	
	Net VAT to be paid to Customs or reclaimed by you **(Difference between boxes 3 and 4)**	**5**	
	Total value of **sales** and all other outputs excluding any VAT. **Include your box 8 figure**	**6**	00
	Total value of **purchases** and all other inputs excluding any VAT. **Include your box 9 figure**	**7**	00
	Total value of all **supplies** of goods and related services, excluding any VAT, to other **EC Member States**	**8**	00
	Total value of all **acquisitions** of goods and related services, excluding any VAT, from other **EC Member States**	**9**	00

Retail schemes. If you have used any of the schemes in the period covered by this return, enter the relevant letter(s) in this box.

If you are enclosing a payment please tick this box.

DECLARATION: You, or someone on your behalf, must sign below.

I,..declare that the
(Full name of signatory in BLOCK LETTERS)

information given above is true and complete.

Signature...Date.............19......

A false declaration can result in prosecution.

L

VAT 100

128

Exercise

Have a go at the following exercises. If you can complete Sonny's book-keeping for February, you will certainly know your way around book-keeping using tax point accounting.

During this exercise you will:

- enter receipts
- enter payments
- cross cast your totals
- reconcile the cash
- reconcile the bank
- complete a sales day book
- complete a purchase day book
- complete a VAT return.

Exercise 15 – Entering Receipts in the Cashbook

Complete the income side for Sonny's business for February using the information below, and the blank form on pages 132 and 133. Enter the date, description and total amount first. Then analyse the total across columns 4 to 7 exactly as we did for the previous month. Remember to calculate the VAT on Sales at 7/47 of the total. Note that Sonny sold a machine for £3,000 plus VAT of £525.00. He received the £3,525 in cash, £200 was retained as cash, the remaining £3,325 was banked.

Date	Transaction	Cash Sale (incl VAT)	Credit Sale (incl VAT)	Other Income (incl VAT)
		£	£	£
Feb 1	Cash Sale	1880.00		
3	Cash Sale	3818.75		
3	Credit Sale		587.50	
6	Sale of machinery			3525.00
7	Cash sale	7637.50		
10	Credit sale		2350.00	
11	Cash sale	4700.00		
12	Cash sale	693.25		
14	Credit sale		1175.00	
16	Cash sale	3995.00		
19	Cash sale	3818.75		
23	Credit sale		2761.25	
25	Cash sale	1468.75		
27	Cash sale	587.50		
28	Cash sale	5287.50		

Exercise 16 – Recording Payments in the Cashbook

Enter the following payments on the right hand side of pages 132 and 133. Remember to make entries for both cash payments and bank deposits in the cash payments column (column 10). Put the cheque payments in the bank payments column (column 11), then analyse the expenditure into the other columns. Remember to extract the VAT, where appropriate, which should be entered in the VAT column (column 12). Check your answer with page 170.

Date		Transaction	Amount £	Paid By
Feb	1	Petrol	30.00	Cash
	2	Banking	1880.00	
	3	Jay's Fabrics (Materials)	11162.50	Cheque
	3	Banking	3818.75	
	3	Wages	5292.20	Direct charge
	4	Die Cast Ltd (Materials)	8812.50	Cheque
	6	Tool hire	47.00	Cash
	6	Petrol	30.00	Cash
	7	Advertising	881.25	Cheque
	7	Banking	11550.00	
	9	Stationery	1410.00	Cheque
	10	Banking	2350.00	
	11	Banking	4700.00	
	11	Petrol	30.00	Cash
	12	Banking	693.25	
	13	New machinery	14100.00	Cheque
	14	Banking	1175.00	
	15	Office supplies	615.00	Cheque
	18	Petrol	30.00	Cash
	18	Banking	3995.00	
	19	Banking	3818.75	
	21	Electric drill	49.35	Cash
	23	Banking	2761.25	
	24	Water rates	890.65	Cheque
	25	Banking	1468.75	
	26	Jay's Fabrics	8022.90	Cheque
	27	Petty cash	145.00	Cheque
	27	Office stationery	312.55	Cheque
	28	Banking	5875.00	

Sonny Sunblinds						
Income						
1	2	3	4	5	6	7
Date	Detail	Total	VAT	Cash Sales	Credit Sales	Other Income

February 19xx

Expenditure

8	9	10	11	12	13	14	15	16	17	18	19	20
Date	Detail	Bankings Cash Out	Bank Payments	VAT	Materials	Travel + Petrol	Telephone	Light Heat	Printing Stationery	Wages	Sundries	Bankings

Exercise 17 – Cross Casting

- Add up all the income columns and agree the total income (column 3) with the totals of columns 4 to 7.

- Agree the total of columns 10 & 11 with the totals of columns 12–20.

Check your answer with pages 170 and 171.

Exercise 18 – Reconciling the Cash (Method 1)

Complete the cash reconciliation below. We have given you the opening cash balance.

		£	
	Cash in hand b/fwd from previous period	55.93	
Add	Cash in	_____	(Col 3)
	Total		
Less	Cash out	· · · · · · _____	(Col 10)
	Cash Balance c/fwd to next period	_____	

Check your answer with page 171.

Exercise 18 – Alternative Method of Reconciling the Cash (Method 2)

			£
	Balance b/fwd		55.93
Add	Cash retained		_____
	Total		
Less	Cash expenditure	£	
	Petrol	· · · · · ·	
	Tool hire	· · · · · ·	
	Electric drill	· · · · · ·	
			_____
Cash Balance Carried Forward			_____

Check your answer with page 172.

Exercise 19 – Reconciling the Bank

Prepare a bank reconciliation using the bank statement shown below and the pro-forma on page 136. The reconciliation period is 1 February to 28 February. We have given you the opening balance.

Date	Particulars	Payments £	Receipts £	Balance £
Feb 1	Opening Balance			31932.43
Feb 1	Sundry credit		14687.50	46619.93
1	Sundry credit		587.50	47207.43
1	Die Cast Ltd	6580.00		40627.43
2	Road Fund Licence	135.00		40492.43
2	Sundry credit		1880.00	42372.43
3	Wages	5292.20		37080.23
3	Sundry credit		3818.75	40898.98
5	Jay's Fabrics	11162.50		29736.48
7	Die Cast Ltd	8812.50		20923.98
7	Sundry credit		11550.00	32473.98
9	Advertising	881.25		31592.73
10	Sundry credit		2350.00	33942.73
11	Stationery	1410.00		32532.73
11	Sundry credit		4700.00	37232.73
12	Sundry credit		693.25	37925.98
14	Sundry credit		1175.00	39100.98
16	New machinery	14100.00		25000.98
18	Sundry credit		3995.00	28995.98
18	Office supplies	615.00		28380.98
19	Sundry credit		3818.75	32199.73
23	Sundry credit		2761.25	34960.98
25	Sundry credit		1468.75	36429.73
27	Water rates	890.65		35539.08
27	Petty cash	145.00		35394.08
	Closing Balance c/fwd			35394.08

Bank Statement – Sonny Sunblinds

Exercise 19 (contd)

Bank Reconciliation at 28 February

	£
Balance per Statement at 28 February	**35394.08**

Add   Banking not shown on statement

	£

Less   Unpresented cheques

. . . .

. . . .

Balance as per Cashbook c/fwd

_____

_____

You can double check the balance which should appear in the cashbook as follows:

Opening balance per cashbook – Jan   . . . . . .

Add   Total bankings per cashbook

_____

. . . . . .

Less   Total bank payments per cashbook   _____

Balance c/fwd on Cashbook

_____

Check your answers with page 172.

Exercise 20 – Sales Day Book

During February, Sonny issued the following sales invoices. Enter these on the blank sales day book sheet on page 138. We have provided the gross invoice value so you will have to extract the VAT element using the VAT fraction.

Date	Customer	Inv No	Gross	Cash Sale	Credit Sale	Date Paid
			£			
Feb 3	Sunspot Ltd	1001	587.50	✓		
4	Sunspot Ltd	1002	3160.75		✓	
6	Venetian Ways	1003	4230.00		✓	19/3/9x
7	Shady Dealings	1004	7637.50	✓		
8	Eclipse Blinds	1005	1504.00		✓	
11	Shadowlands	1006	4700.00	✓		
12	Sunshield Blinds	1007	5722.25		✓	
16	Blind Love	1018	3995.00	✓		
23	The Sunblind Co	1009	2761.25	✓		
24	Eclipse Blinds	1010	705.00		✓	

Check your answer with page 173.

Sales Day Book

Date	Customer	Inv No	Gross Amount	VAT	Cash Sales (net)	Credit Sales (net)	Date Paid	Remarks
Totals								

Exercise 21 – Purchase Day Book

During February, Sonny received the following purchase invoices. Enter these purchase invoices on the blank purchase day book sheet on page 140. We have provided the gross invoice value so you will have to compute the VAT element using the VAT fraction.

Date		Supplier	Ref No	Gross	Date Paid	Description
				£		
Feb	1	Petrol	150	30.00	1/2/199x	Motor
	3	Jay's Fabrics	151	11162.50	3/2/199x	Stock
	4	Die Cast Ltd	152	8812.50	4/2/199x	Stock
	6	Tool hire	153	47.00	6/2/199x	Other
	6	Petrol	154	30.00	6/2/199x	Motor
	7	The Advertiser	155	881.50	7/2/199x	Other
	9	Office Supply Co	156	1410.00	9/2/199x	Stationery
	11	Petrol	157	30.00	11/2/199x	Motor
	15	Office Supply Co	158	615.00	15/2/199x	Stationery
	18	Petrol	159	30.00	18/2/199x	Motor
	21	Electric drill	160	49.35	21/2/199x	Other
	24	Water Rates	161	890.65	24/2/199x	Other
	26	Jay's Fabrics	162	8022.90	26/2/199x	Stock
	27	Office Supply Co	163	312.55	27/2/199x	Stationery

Check your answer with page 174.

Purchase Day Book

1 Date	2 Supplier	3 Ref No	4 Gross Amt	5 VAT	6 Net Amt	7 Date Paid	8 Stock (net)	9 Motor (net)	10 Tel (net)	11 Stat (net)	12 Other (net)	

Exercise 22 – Completing the VAT Return

Using the purchase and sales day books that you have just completed for February, work out Sonny's VAT return using the blank on page 142. Remember that you would normally complete a VAT return quarterly but, for practice, just use February's figures. You will also need to make an adjustment for a fuel scale charge as Sonny uses his car for both business and private motoring and reclaims the input VAT. We will assume Sonny has a petrol car which is 1900 cc.

The scale charge for one month would be:

Gross Scale Charge	VAT	Net Scale Charge
£74	£11.02	£63.00 (rounded up)

VAT Return Entries

£

Output Tax	. . . .	(Box 1)
Input Tax	. . . .	(Box 4)
Due to HMC&E	. . . . . .	(Box 5)
Sales Outputs	. . . .	(Box 6)
Purchase Inputs	. . . . . .	(Box 7)

Check your answer with page 175.

Exercise 23 – Balancing the Books

When you have completed entries, balance the book along the lines shown on page 115.

Check your answer with page 176.

Value Added Tax Return

For the period

HM Customs
and Excise

Exercise 23 (contd)

Your VAT Office telephone number is

For Official Use

Registration Number   Period

You could be liable to a financial penalty it your completed return and all the VAT payable are not received by the due date.

Due date:

For Official Use

Before you fill in this form please read the notes on the back and the VAT leaflet *"Filling in your VAT return"*. Fill in all boxes clearly in ink, and write 'none' where necessary. Don't put a dash or leave any box blank. If there are no pence write "**00**" in the pence column. **Do not** enter more than one amount in any box.

For official use		£	p
	VAT due in this period on **sales** and other outputs **1**		
	VAT due in this period on **acquisitions** from other **EC Member States** **2**		
	Total VAT due (**the sum of boxes 1 and 2**) **3**		
	VAT reclaimed in this period on **purchases** and other inputs (including acquisitions from the EC) **4**		
	Net VAT to be paid to Customs or reclaimed by you (**Difference between boxes 3 and 4**) **5**		
	Total value of **sales** and all other outputs excluding any VAT. **Include your box 8 figure** **6**		00
	Total value of **purchases** and all other inputs excluding any VAT. **Include your box 9 figure** **7**		00
	Total value of all **supplies** of goods and related services, excluding any VAT, to other **EC Member States** **8**		00
	Total value of all **acquisitions** of goods and related services, excluding any VAT, from other **EC Member States** **9**		00
	Retail schemes. If you have used any of the schemes in the period covered by this return, enter the relevant letter(s) in this box.		

If you are enclosing a payment please tick this box.

DECLARATION: You, or someone on your behalf, must sign below.

I,..declare that the
(Full name of signatory in BLOCK LETTERS)

information given above is true and complete.

Signature...Date.............19......

A false declaration can result in prosecution.

L

VAT 100

Chapter 7

Filing Your Records

Whatever book-keeping system you use, you must file all sales invoices, purchase invoices, wages records, cash receipts etc. This is because:

- you may need to refer to them if you have a dispute with a customer or supplier.

- your VAT inspector will ask to see a representative sample of invoices. 'Sod's Law' will dictate that he asks for the ones you haven't filed away. If you've filed everything, you should be in a good position to respond.

Before!

- you could be asked to produce your records in the event of a dispute with the Inland Revenue.

- your accountant will want to see these records when he conducts his audit and prepares the accounts for submission to the Inland Revenue.

- by law you are required to retain records for a period of six years.

The number and type of records you possess will depend upon the complexity of your business. Cash traders will have less to file than traders giving credit.

Even small traders will normally need to keep copies of their sales invoices (or till roll), purchase invoices, petty cash, bank statements and wages sheets, where applicable. Traders who give, or

After!

receive, credit will also need a sales day book (particularly if VAT registered) and, possibly, purchase ledger cards. The following notes summarise the filing records that you could be required to maintain. A flow diagram at the end of the section shows how they all link into the analysed cashbook.

Till Rolls

If you are a retailer, you must keep your till rolls. They are an important source of book-keeping information. The daily takings in your cashbook will be made up from information on the till rolls. Keep them in date order.

Sales Invoice File

If you sell items on credit, it is essential to keep a copy of all sales invoices sent to customers.

These can be kept in an ordinary ring binder. Punch two holes in the duplicate copy of the sales invoice and put it into the 'Unpaid Sales Invoices' ring binder. Do this immediately after it is typed. Avoid the temptation to file the invoices at a later date. If the invoices are filed immediately, they cannot get lost.

Remember to number each invoice sequentially. Clearly describe the goods despatched or the service performed and show the VAT you have added. Some customers use an incomplete invoice as a reason for delaying payment.

When an invoice is paid, transfer it to another ring binder clearly labelled 'Paid Sales Invoices'. Write the date and number of the cheque you receive on the invoice.

By using this simple system, no invoice should get lost because it will be filed immediately it is typed. All unpaid invoices come quickly to hand because they are in date order. File paid sales invoices in invoice number order. This will make it easy to trace old invoices should it be necessary.

If only part payment of an invoice is received, write on the invoice the amount you have received but *do not* transfer it into the 'Paid' file until it has been fully paid.

Sales Day Book

We have seen an example of a sales day book in the previous section. If used, it can include a range of information including:

- date
- invoice number
- customer's name
- gross amount
- VAT amount
- net amount
- a 'paid' column (which can be ticked or dated on payment)
- a column for remarks.

Sales Ledger Cards

If you have a lot of credit customers, you may need to send them statements. A statement is a list of all outstanding invoices. If you send statements, you will have to keep a detailed record of each customer's account. This can be done on a Sales Ledger Card. Every time an invoice is raised, it is entered on the card. When the invoice is paid, the entry is cancelled. This can be a time consuming chore to do manually. If you have a lot of credit customers, you should consider a computerised accounting system.

Purchase Invoice File

File your purchase invoices as soon as they are received in an 'Unpaid Purchase Invoices' file. This ensures that the invoice cannot get lost. To help find invoices in the future, allocate a serial reference number of your own. This can be written on the invoice in red ink. Keep delivery notes and credit notes in the same file. Attach them to the invoice when it is sent to you.

Special stamping machines are available to label large numbers of purchase invoices.

When the invoice is paid, transfer it to a 'Paid Purchase Invoices' file. This means that there is never any doubt about how much is owed and to whom. When you pay an invoice, write your cheque number on the invoice. This provides an important link between your banking records and your purchase records.

If only part payment of an invoice is made, write on the invoice the amount you have paid but *do not* transfer it into the 'Paid' file until it has been fully paid.

Purchase Day Book

We have seen an example of a purchase day book in the previous section. If used, it can contain the following information:

- date on supplier's invoice
- supplier's name
- supplier's invoice number
- your reference number (serial)
- gross amount (including VAT)

- VAT amount
- net amount
- a column to indicate date paid.

Purchase Ledger Cards

If you have enough purchase invoices, you may want to keep a summary of your dealings with each supplier. Every supplier can be allocated a card. Purchase invoices are logged onto the card when received and logged when paid. This is a chore if you have to do it by hand. If you have a lot of suppliers you should consider a computerised accounting system.

Banking Records

It is important to keep track of your bank position. Ask your bank to send you a monthly statement. These can be kept in a ring binder or one of the special folders issued by the bank.

Now that banks do not return used cheques, it is important that you fill in cheque counterfoils and retain them. They should be filed in an envelope or special (small) drawer as they are easily lost. Cheque stubs may be your best link between an amount paid by cheque and the goods/services to which they relate. Enter the supplier's invoice number and any reference number you may devise as well as the name, date etc on the counterfoil.

Keep your bank paying-in book to hand. This will enable you to check that cheques have been entered correctly into your account.

Wages Sheets

Whether you choose to devise your own wages sheet or use Form P11 supplied by the Inland Revenue, you will need to keep records of gross wages, tax deducted, national insurance paid, pension contributions etc. These are probably best kept on wages sheets that can be filed in a loose-leaf wages book. It may help if the wages book has a pocket to keep the instructions, tables and leaflets issued by the Inland Revenue and Department of Social Security. Bound wages books can be purchased from stationers quite cheaply should you prefer to use them.

Petty Cash

In order to save your analysed cashbook from unnecessary clutter, many people operate a Petty Cash Book.

This book contains details of very small amounts of money spent. Totals from the petty cash book are periodically transferred to the analysed cashbook when there are sufficient entries to make this worthwhile. Many people operate the 'imprest' system of controlling petty cash. This is explained in Chapter 8.

Credit Card Payments

You may choose to pay for some items with a credit card. Keep all of your credit card slips in a binder and check them off against the credit card statement when it arrives. Split the credit card expenditures across the headings in your analysed cashbook in much the same way as you would account for petty cash.

Receipts for Cash Spent by You

It is important to keep all cash receipts because:

- they form part of your records

- they are evidence of your purchase in the event of a dispute with your supplier

- they may be requested by the VAT inspector

- they could, possibly, be required by the income tax inspector.

Again, a simple ring binder should be sufficient for your needs. According to the number and type of receipts, you may decide to classify them by source of purchase, otherwise date order should suffice. Small receipts can be stapled to a page and labelled with type or date of purchase.

Record of Cash Received

You will need some record of cash received. If you have a lot of cash receipts, you will probably install a till so that amounts are automatically recorded. If you have a few cash receipts, you will probably only keep a record of daily totals.

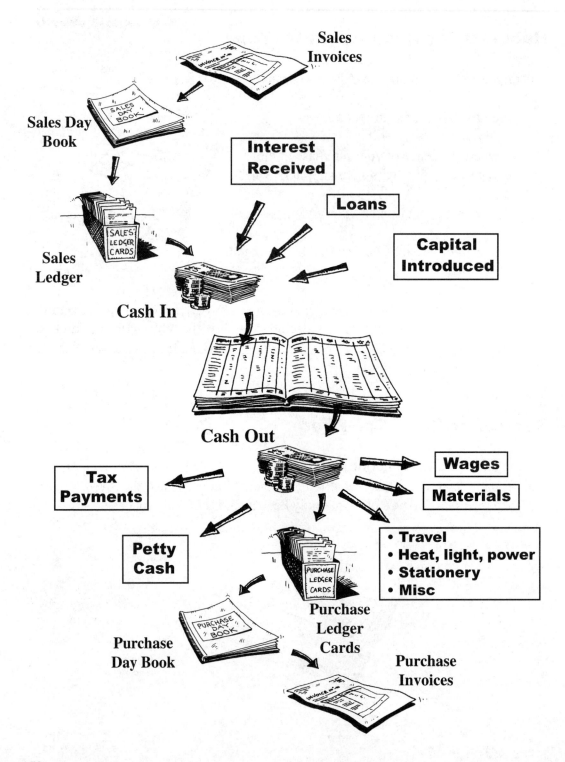

Sales Invoices

Sales Day Book

Interest Received

Loans

Capital Introduced

Sales Ledger

Cash In

Cash Out

Tax Payments

Wages

Materials

- Travel
- Heat, light, power
- Stationery
- Misc

Petty Cash

Purchase Ledger Cards

Purchase Day Book

Purchase Invoices

Chapter 8

Petty Cash

Most businesses pay out small sums on items such as tea, coffee, milk, stamps, petrol etc. Often these items are paid for in cash. Accounting for small amounts of cash can be a nightmare because people often take money out of cash takings without recording the withdrawal. Sometimes they think that the amount is so small that it's hardly worth bothering to record in the cashbook. Even though the individual sums are small, over the course of the trading year they can amount to a lot. A great deal of valuable time can be spent trying to track down small amounts of cash after the event.

Even when staff are careful to collect receipts for petty cash, you can still have problems. For example, a person could purchase tea and coffee with money taken from the till. At the end of the day, the till is cashed up and the takings recorded. Chances are the takings will not be grossed up to include the amount of money taken out to pay for the tea and coffee. This will lead to an under-recording on takings. This can cause problems when trying to reconcile cash later on.

From a security and audit point of view, it is far better to bank the day's takings intact. This gives you a record of bankings that agrees with the till roll and cashbook. If we bank the entire day's takings, we obviously need a petty cash system that doesn't involve taking cash out of the till. One very good system is called the Imprest System. This is described over the page.

The Imprest System

The Imprest System is an effective way to control petty cash, it also minimises the number of entries you need to make in your analysis book. The system works as follows.

A certain sum of money, say £100, is chosen as the 'imprest' balance. This sum is chosen because it is enough to meet the petty cash needs of, say, a week or a month. The £100 cash is put into a tin or other receptacle. As money is taken to pay for items, the receipts are put back into the imprest tin. The sum of the receipts plus cash must always add back to the original imprest balance. When cash gets low, the imprest is 'topped up' to the original imprest level by exchanging the receipts for cash drawn from the bank. This simple system has the following advantages.

- There is always a limited amount of money in the petty cash tin. This limits the amount of loss should a theft occur.

- Theft can be detected easily since the sum of receipts plus cash must always add back to the imprest amount.

- The number of entries in the analysed cashbook are reduced to a minimum. An entry is only made when the imprest is topped up.

- Petty cash can be collected together and accounted for in one place by one person.

When it is time to top up the imprest, take out the receipts and record them as follows.

Petty Cash Records

You will want to keep petty cash records because:

- You want to reclaim the VAT on petty cash. To do this, you need a system which records the VAT relief that you are entitled to.

- Over the course of a year, petty cash could amount to a sizeable amount. You may want to examine the records periodically.

- Your accountant or tax inspector could ask to see your petty cash records. They know that petty cash is sometimes a dumping ground for all sorts of minor problems and indiscretions!

On page 154 we have shown an example of a petty cash sheet using the imprest system. As you can see, it looks like a simplified analysed cashbook sheet. It has 'cash in' on the left hand side and expenditure on the right hand side. We suggest that you draw up one of these sheets with expenditure headings to suit your business. Note that we have added a column to enable you to number your petty cash vouchers. This is optional but it will assist you in tracing receipts should you be asked to produce them.

In our example, we have included a VAT column as we are assuming the trader is VAT registered. This column ensures that we don't forget to reclaim VAT relief to which we are entitled. You will need to:

- add the amount of VAT to be reclaimed into box 4 of your VAT return
- adjust box 7 to include the total amount spent on petty cash, net of VAT.

If you are not registered for VAT then you do not need a separate VAT column. All items of expenditure on the cash sheet can be entered gross.

On the left hand side of the petty cash sheet you will see that we start off with £100 as our opening imprest balance. We have then entered each item paid out of petty cash. We have shown the date, detail, petty cash voucher number and the total expenditure. As you can see, we have then sub-analysed this expenditure across various headings. In our example, the petty cash sheet is prepared on a weekly basis but this can, of course, be prepared over whatever period you choose. At the end of the week, add up all the receipts in the tin. In our example, the total comes to £77.87 so we need to draw a cheque on the bank for this amount to bring the petty cash balance back to the original £100. This then forms the opening balance for the following week.

Weekly Petty Cash Sheet

Receipts	Date	Detail	Petty Cash Voucher	Total	Post/ Station- ery	Travel	Clean- ing	Misc	Enter- taining	VAT
100.00	1.1.199x	Imprest-Top up								
	1.1.199x	Tea/coffee	001	6.25			6.25			
	2.1.199x	Stationery	002	9.87	8.40					1.47
	2.1.199x	Bus fare	003	1.60		1.60				
	3.1.199x	Window cleaner	004	6.50			6.50			
	3.1.199x	Petrol	005	10.00		8.51				1.49
	3.1.199x	Stamps	006	4.40	4.40					
	4.1.199x	Stationery	007	7.05	6.00					1.05
	5.1.199x	Petrol	008	10.00		8.51				1.49
	5.1.199x	Entertaining/ Meal out	009	18.80					18.80	
	5.1.199x	Milk	010	3.40				3.40		
22.13			Totals	77.87						
77.87			Balance	22.13						
100.00	7.1.199x	Imprest-Top up								

154

Reconciling Cash and Petty Cash

If we use the imprest system, we must still be able to reconcile our cash exactly as before. This is important because cash reconciliation helps ensure the integrity of the book-keeping system. If we operate an imprest system, some of our cash is stored in the petty cash tin. This can make cash reconciliation slightly more complicated. To keep things simple we suggest you use the following routine. You can deviate from this method later on when you feel more confident.

- On the last day of the month, have a look in the petty cash tin. See how much cash is required to bring the petty cash back to the imprest amount.

- Cash a cheque with the bank for this amount. Put the cash in the tin and remove the receipts (the receipts should of course add up to the amount of cash you have just put in the tin).

- Analyse the receipts onto a petty cash sheet along the lines of the example on page 154. Put the receipts in a safe place and cross reference them to the petty cash sheet that you have just completed.

- Make an entry in the 'bank payments' column for the total amount used to top up the imprest. If your petty cash is spent on a few low value items then you may decide to allocate the whole of the imprest top up to the 'sundries' column. However, if you use large amounts of petty cash to pay for items like petrol, then you should allocate petrol costs to the 'travel' column and only put the balance to the sundries column.

- Your treatment of VAT will depend on your VAT registration 'status'. If you are not VAT registered then obviously you can treat all petty cash expenditures as gross expenditures because you will not be able to reclaim the VAT. If you are a cash accounting trader, we suggest that you enter the VAT in your cashbook exactly as you would for a normal cash accounting transaction. If you are on invoice accounting, we suggest that you extract the VAT from your petty cash sheets quarterly at the same time as you examine your sales and purchase day books.

- If you operate the system we suggest, you will find that your cash reconciliation is very simple indeed. Since you open and close every month with the imprest balance intact in your petty cash tin (it is intact because you have just topped it up!) you simply have to add the imprest amount to the amount calculated in your normal cash reconciliation. You don't need to show any entries for 'petty cash in' and 'petty cash out' because these are covered by 'bank payments' whenever a imprest top up is made.

Model Answers

Let's see how well you have done!

Answer to Exercise 1 (page 18)

Calculate the VAT included in the following VAT inclusive prices

£ 150	x	$\frac{7}{47}$	=	£22.34
£ 290	x	$\frac{7}{47}$	=	£43.19
£ 56	x	$\frac{7}{47}$	=	£8.34
£ 2,670	x	$\frac{7}{47}$	=	£397.66

Answer to Exercise 2 (page 42)   See overleaf.

Answer to Exercise 2 (page 42)

David and Jean — December 19xx

Income

1 Date	2 Detail	3 Cash In	4 Cheques In	5 Sales	6 Other
	Cash Balance B/F	70.35			
Jan 2	Table		162.50	162.50	
5	Settee		142.25	142.25	
10	Bookshelves		235.00	235.00	
14	Timber	40.00		40.00	
19	Capital Introduced		400.00		400.00
19	Bookcase		85.00	85.00	
27	Desk		421.00	421.00	
28	Old clock		190.00	190.00	
	Totals	40.00	1637.75	1275.75	400.00

£1675.75 £1675.75

(Including B/F) 110.35

Expenditure

7 Date	8 Detail	9 Cash Spent	10 Cash to Bank	11 Bank Payments	12 Materials	13 Phone + Postage	14 Motor Expenses	15 Sundries	16 Bank Deposits
	Bank Balance B/F								302.50
Jan 2	Postage stamps	8.00				8.00			
6	T Jones (materials)			140.00	140.00				
6	Banking		304.75						304.75
10	S Roberts (materials)			259.00	259.00				
11	Banking		235.00						235.00
14	Petrol	25.00					25.00		
19	Banking		485.00						485.00
20	Rates			523.64				523.64	
20	Electricity			98.33				98.33	
20	Gas			204.25				204.25	
22	Tea/coffee	4.74						4.74	
30	Banking		611.00						611.00
30	Drawings			300.00				300.00	
30	Stationery	1.33						1.33	
	Totals	39.07	1635.75	1525.22	399.00	8.00	25.00	1132.29	1635.75
	Bank Bal C/F			413.03					1938.25
	Cash Bal C/F	71.28							

£3200.04 £3200.04

110.35   1938.25

Annotations:
- Cross casting this month's income excluding brought forward amount
- 'Cash In' equals 'Cash Out'
- Cross casting this month's expenditure excluding brought forward amount
- 'Bank In' equals 'Bank Out'
- 110.35
- 1938.25

Answer to Exercise 3 (page 43)

Income	£	£
Column 3	40.00	
Column 4	1635.75	
Total Columns 3–4		**1675.75**
Column 5	1275.75	
Column 6	400.00	
Total Columns 5–6		**1675.75**

Expenditure	£	£
Column 9	39.07	
Column 10	1635.75	
Column 11	1525.22	
Total Columns 9–11		**3200.04**
Column 12	399.00	
Column 13	8.00	
Column 14	25.00	
Column 15	1132.29	
Column 16	1635.75	
Total Columns 12–16		**3200.04**

Answer to Exercise 4 (page 43)

	£
Cash Balance b/fwd from Dec	70.35
Add Cash received per Cashbook	40.00
	110.35
Less Cash payments per Cashbook	39.07
Cash Balance c/fwd to Feb	71.28

Answer to Exercise 5 (pages 46 and 47)

Reconciling the Bank

Bank Balance as per Cashbook

		£
Reconciled bank balance b/f		302.50
Add Bank deposits		1635.75
		1938.25
Less Bank payments		1525.22
Balance as per Cashbook		413.03

Bank Balance as per Bank Statement

Cashbook items not on Bank Statement include:

30 Jan	Banking	£611
30 Jan	Drawing	£300

	£
Balance as per bank statement	102.03
Add Unrecorded banking	611.00
	713.03
Less Unpresented cheque	300.00
Balance as per Cashbook	413.03

Answer to Exercises 6 and 7 (pages 68 to 70) See page 165

Appendix 1

Answer to Exercises 6 and 7 (pages 68 to 72)

Hardcastle's Hardware — February 19xx

Income

1 Date	2 Detail	3 Total In	4 VAT	5 Sales	6 Other Income	7
	Cash Bal B/fwd	50 00				
Feb 1	Sales	246 45	36 71	209 74		
1	Sales	558 12	83 12	475 00		
3	Sales	312 94	46 61	266 33		
6	Sales	185 46	27 62	157 84		
10	Sales	194 74	29 00	165 74		
15	Sales	321 89	47 94	273 95		
18	Sales	218 95	32 61	186 34		
19	Sales	314 58	46 85	267 73		
19	Sale of Van	117 50	17 50		100 00	
22	Sales	134 58	20 04	114 54		
24	Sales	215 69	32 12	183 57		
24	Sales	352 50	52 50	300 00		
25	Sales	216 78	32 29	184 49		
26	Sales	358 74	53 43	305 31		
28	Sales	421 64	62 80	358 84		
		4170 56	621 14	3449 42	100 00	
		£4170.56				
(Including B/F)		4220 56				

'Cash in' equals 'Cash out'

Expenditure

8 Date	9 Detail	10 To Bank	11 Bank Payments	12 VAT	13 Materials	14 Travel + Petrol	15 Telephone	16 Light Heat	17 Printing Stationery	18 Wages	19 Sundries	20 Bankings
	Bank Bal B/fwd											2069 55
Feb 1	Building Supplies		423 65	63 10	360 55							
1	Acme Paint Co		258 96	38 57	220 39							
2	Wages		135 00							135 00		
3	Banking	246 45										246 45
6	Banking	558 12										558 12
6	Banking	312 94										312 94
10	Gas		125 94	18 76				107 18				
10	Banking	185 46										185 46
15	Banking	194 74										194 74
15	Red Brick Co		321 65	47 91	273 74							
15	Telephone		81 05	12 07			68 98					
18	Bank Charges		20 00								20 00	
18	Banking	321 89										321 89
19	Banking	218 95										218 95
22	Banking	432 08										432 08
24	Banking	134 58										134 58
25	Banking	568 19										568 19
25	The Hardware Co		824 23	122 76	701 47							
26	Drawings		500 00								500 00	
26	Banking	216 78										216 78
27	Banking	358 74										358 74
28	Banking	421 64										421 64
28	Petty cash		72 32	9 28		42 56			10 52		9 96	
		4170 56	2762 80	312 45	1556 15	42 56	68 98	107 18	10 52	135 00	529 96	4170 56
		£6933.36	**£6933.36**									
	Cash Bal C/F	50 00										
	Bank Bal C/F		3477 31									
(Including B/F)		4220 56	6240 11									6240 11

'Bank in' equals 'Bank out'

161

Answer to Exercise 8 (page 71)   Cross Casting

Income

	£	£
Column 4	621.14	
Column 5	3449.42	
Column 6	100.00	
Total Columns 4–7		**4170.56**
Total Column 3		**4170.56**

Expenditure

	£	£
Column 10	4170.56	
Column 11	2762.80	
Total Columns 10 + 11		**6933.36**
Column 12	312.45	
Column 13	1556.15	
Column 14	42.56	
Column 15	68.98	
Column 16	107.18	
Column 17	10.52	
Column 18	135.00	
Column 19	529.96	
Column 20	4170.56	
Total Columns 12–20		**6933.36**

Answer to Exercise 9 (page 71) Reconciling the Bank

	£
Cash b/fwd from previous period	50.00
Add Income	4170.56
	4220.56
Less Bankings	4170.56
Cash carried forward to next period	50.00

Answer to Exercise 10 (pages 74 and 75)

Reconciling the Bank

Bank Balance as per Cashbook

		£
	Reconciled bank balance b/fwd	2069.55
Add	Bank deposits	4170.56
		6240.11
Less	Bank payments	2762.80
	Balance as per Cashbook	3447.31

Bank Balance per Bank Statement

		£
	Bank balance as per bank statement	3627.99
Add	Unrecorded banking	421.64
		4049.63
Less	Unpresented cheque	572.32
	Reconciled bank balance c/fwd	3477.31

Answer to Exercise 11 (page 76)

Calculation of VAT Due

	£	
Sales Output Tax	621.14	}(box 1)
VAT due per Car	13.25	
Purchases Input Tax	(312.45)	(box 4)
Amount due to HMC&E	321.94	(box 5)

Value of Sales Outputs

Sales	3449.00	
Net of VAT scale charges	76.00	
Sale of Van	100.00	
Total	3625.00	(box 6)

Value of Purchase Inputs

Materials	1556.00	
Travel/Motor	43.00	
Telephone	69.00	
Light and heat	107.00	
Printing and stationery	11.00	
Sundries Post/tea	10.00	
Total	1796.00	(box 7)

Value Added Tax Return

For the period

For Official Use

HM Customs
and Excise

**Answer to Exercise 11 (contd)
(page 77)**

Registration Number	Period

You could be liable to a financial penalty it your completed return and all the VAT payable are not received by the due date.

Due date:

For Official Use	

Your VAT Office telephone number is

Before you fill in this form please read the notes on the back and the VAT leaflet *"Filling in your VAT return"*. Fill in all boxes clearly in ink, and write 'none' where necessary. Don't put a dash or leave any box blank. If there are no pence write **"00"** in the pence column. **Do not** enter more than one amount in any box.

For official use			£	p
	VAT due in this period on **sales** and other outputs	1	634	39
	VAT due in this period on **acquisitions** from other **EC Member States**	2	None	
	Total VAT due **(the sum of boxes 1 and 2)**	3	634	39
	VAT reclaimed in this period on **purchases** and other inputs (including acquisitions from the EC)	4	312	45
	Net VAT to be paid to Customs or reclaimed by you **(Difference between boxes 3 and 4)**	5	321	94
	Total value of **sales** and all other outputs excluding any VAT. **Include your box 8 figure**	6	3625	00
	Total value of **purchases** and all other inputs excluding any VAT. **Include your box 9 figure**	7	1796	00
	Total value of all **supplies** of goods and related services, excluding any VAT, to other **EC Member States**	8	None	00
	Total value of all **acquisitions** of goods and related services, excluding any VAT, from other **EC Member States**	9	None	00

Retail schemes. If you have used any of the schemes in the period covered by this return, enter the relevant letter(s) in this box.

If you are enclosing a payment please tick this box.

DECLARATION: You, or someone on your behalf, must sign below.

I,..declare that the
(Full name of signatory in BLOCK LETTERS)

information given above is true and complete.

Signature...Date..............19......

A false declaration can result in prosecution.

L

VAT 100

Answer to Exercise 12 (pages 103 to 104)

Sales Day Book

Date	Customer	Inv No	Gross Amount	VAT	Cash Sales Net	Credit Sales Net	Date Paid	Remarks
1/3/199x	J Smith	121	235.00	35.00		200.00	1/4/9x	
1/3/199x	Cash Sales		564.05	84.01	480.04			
2/3/199x	W Smith	122	381.87	56.87		325.00	10/4/9x	
2/3/199x	Cash Sales		425.97	63.44	362.53			
3/3/199x	S Robins	123	440.63	65.63		375.00	15/4/9x	
3/3/199x	Cash Sales		294.58	43.87	250.71			
4/3/199x	D Rees	124	235.00	35.00		200.00		Still owing at 20/4/9x
4/3/199x	Cash Sales		356.98	53.17	303.81			
5/3/199x	D Power	125	117.50	17.50		100.00	21/3/9x	
5/3/199x	Cash Sales		521.45	77.66	443.79			
Totals			3573.03	532.15	1840.88	1200.00		

Answer to Exercise 12 (pages 107 to 108)

Purchase Day Book

Date	Supplier	Ref No	Gross Amt	VAT	Net Amt	Date Paid	Stock (net)	Motor (net)	Tel (net)	Stat (net)	Other (net)
1/3/199x	D Roberts	101	117.50	17.50	100.00	25/4/9x	100.00				
1/3/199x	Petrol	102	20.00	2.98	17.02	1/3/9x		17.02			
1/3/199x	Print Co	103	58.75	8.75	50.00					50.00	
2/3/199x	T Brown	104	256.98	38.27	218.71	31/3/9x	218.71				
2/3/199x	Telephone	105	98.86	14.72	84.14	31/3/9x			84.14		
2/3/199x	Petrol	106	25.00	3.72	21.28	2/3/9x		21.28			
3/3/199x	J Jones	107	545.62	81.26	464.36	15/4/9x	464.36				
3/3/199x	Repairs	108	62.23	9.27	52.96	3/3/9x					59.26
4/3/199x	D S Ben	109	22.36	3.33	19.03	4/3/9x	19.03				
5/3/199x	Postage	110	10.00	0.00	10.00	5/3/9x					10.00
5/3/199x	Garage	111	58.46	8.71	49.75	5/3/9x		49.75			
Totals			1275.76	188.51	1087.25		802.10	88.05	84.14	50.00	62.96

Answer to Exercise 14 (page 127)

	£	
Output Tax	532.15	(box 1)
Input Tax	188.51	(box 4)
Due to HMC&E:	343.64	(box 5)

Sales Outputs:

Cash Sales	1841.00	
Credit Sales	1200.00	
Total Sales Outputs	3041.00	(box 6)

Purchase Inputs: 1087.00   (box 7)

These figures are entered on the VAT form 100 on page 169.

Value Added Tax Return

For the period

HM Customs and Excise crest

HM Customs
and Excise

Answer to Exercise 14 (contd)
(page 128)

Your VAT Office telephone number is

For Official Use	

Registration Number	Period

You could be liable to a financial penalty it your completed return and all the VAT payable are not received by the due date.

Due date:

For Official Use	

Before you fill in this form please read the notes on the back and the VAT leaflet *"Filling in your VAT return"*. Fill in all boxes clearly in ink, and write 'none' where necessary. Don't put a dash or leave any box blank. If there are no pence write **"00"** in the pence column. **Do not** enter more than one amount in any box.

For official use		£	p
	VAT due in this period on **sales** and other outputs **1**	532	15
	VAT due in this period on **acquisitions** from other **EC Member States** **2**	None	
	Total VAT due **(the sum of boxes 1 and 2)** **3**	532	15
	VAT reclaimed in this period on **purchases** and other inputs (including acquisitions from the EC) **4**	188	51
	Net VAT to be paid to Customs or reclaimed by you **(Difference between boxes 3 and 4)** **5**	343	64
	Total value of **sales** and all other outputs excluding any VAT. **Include your box 8 figure** **6**	3041	00
	Total value of **purchases** and all other inputs excluding any VAT. **Include your box 9 figure** **7**	1087	00
	Total value of all **supplies** of goods and related services, excluding any VAT, to other **EC Member States** **8**	None	00
	Total value of all **acquisitions** of goods and related services, excluding any VAT, from other **EC Member States** **9**	None	00

Retail schemes. If you have used any of the schemes in the period covered by this return, enter the relevant letter(s) in this box.

If you are enclosing a payment please tick this box.

DECLARATION: You, or someone on your behalf, must sign below.

I,...declare that the
(Full name of signatory in BLOCK LETTERS)

information given above is true and complete.

Signature...Date.............19......

A false declaration can result in prosecution.

L

VAT 100

169

Answer to Exercises 15, 16 and 17 (pages 130 to 132)

Sonny Sunblinds

February 19xx

Income

1 Date	2 Detail	3 Total	4 VAT	5 Cash Sales	6 Credit Sales	7 Other Income
Feb 1	Cash Sale	1880 00	280 00	1600 00		
3	Cash Sale	3818 75	568 75	3250 00		
3	Credit Sale	587 50	87 50		500 00	
6	Sale of Machinery	3525 00	525 00			3000 00
7	Cash Sale	7637 50	1137 50	6500 00		
10	Credit Sale	2350 00	350 00		2000 00	
11	Cash Sale	4700 00	700 00	4000 00		
12	Cash Sale	693 25	103 25	590 00		
14	Credit Sale	1175 00	175 00		1000 00	
16	Cash Sale	3995 00	595 00	3400 00		
19	Cash Sale	3818 75	568 75	3250 00		
23	Credit Sale	2761 25	411 25		2350 00	
25	Cash Sale	1468 75	218 75	1250 00		
27	Cash Sale	587 50	87 50	500 00		
28	Cash Sale	5287 50	787 50	4500 00		
	Totals	44285 75	6595 75	28840 00	5850 00	3000 00

44285.75

Expenditure

8 Date	9 Detail	10 Bankings & Cash	11 Bank Payments	12 VAT	13 Materials	14 Travel + Petrol	15 Telephone	16 Light Heat	17 Printing Stationery	18 Wages	19 Sundries	20 Bankings
Feb 1	Petrol	30 00		4 47		25 53						
2	Banking	1880 00										1880 00
3	Jay's Fabrics		11162 50	1662 50	9500 00							
3	Banking	3818 75										3818 75
4	Wages		5292 20							5292 20		
4	Die Cast Ltd		8812 50	1312 50	7500 00							
6	Tool Hire	47 00		7 00							40 00	
6	Petrol	30 00		4 47		25 53						
7	Advertising		881 25	131 25							750 00	
7	Banking	11550 00										11550 00
9	Stationery		1410 00	210 00					1200 00			
10	Banking	2350 00										2350 00
11	Banking	4700 00										4700 00
11	Petrol	30 00		4 47		25 53						
12	Banking	693 25										693 25
13	New Machinery		14100 00	2100 00							12000 00	
14	Banking	1175 00										1175 00
15	Office Supplies		615 00	91 60					523 40			
18	Petrol	30 00		4 47		25 53						
18	Banking	3995 00										3995 00
19	Banking	3818 75										3818 75
21	Electric Drill		49 35	7 35							42 00	
23	Banking	2761 25										2761 25
24	Water Rates		890 65								890 65	
25	Banking	1468 75										1468 75
26	Jay's Fabrics		8022 90	1194 90	6828 00							
27	Petty Cash		145 00								145 00	
27	Office Stationery		312 55	46 55					266 00			
28	Banking	5875 00										5875 00
	Totals	44302 10	51644 55	6781 53	23828 00	102 12			1989 40	5292 20	13867 65	44085 75

95946.65

95946.65

Answer to Exercise 17 (page 134)

Income	£	£
Total Column 3		**44285.75**
Column 4	6595.75	
Column 5	28840.00	
Column 6	5850.00	
Column 7	3000.00	
Total Columns 4–7		**44285.75**

Expenditure		
Column 10	44302.10	
Column 11	51644.55	
Total Columns 10–11		**95946.65**
Column 12	6781.53	
Column 13	23828.00	
Column 14	102.12	
Column 15	None	
Column 16	None	
Column 17	1989.40	
Column 18	5292.20	
Column 19	13867.65	
Column 20	44085.75	
Total Columns 12–20		**95946.65**

Answer to Exercise 18 (page 134) – Reconciling the Cash (Method 1)

		£
	Cash b/fwd from previous period	55.93
Add	Cash in	44285.75 (Column 3)
		44341.68
Less	Cash out	44302.10 (Column 10)
	Cash c/fwd to next period	39.58

Answer to Exercise 18 (page 134) – Alternative Method of Reconciling the Cash (Method 2)

			£
	Balance b/fwd		55.93
Add	Cash retained		200.00
	Total		255.93
Less	Cash expenditure	£	
	Petrol	120.00	
	Tool hire	47.00	
	Electric drill	49.35	
			216.35
	Cash Balance Carried Forward		39.58

Answer to Exercise 19 (pages 135 and 136)

			£
	Balance per statement at 28 February		35394.08
Add	Banking not shown on statement		5875.00
			41269.08
Less	Unpresented cheques	£	
	Feb 26 Jay's Fabrics	8022.90	
	Feb 27 Office stationery	312.55	
			8335.45
	Bank balance c/fwd		**32933.63**

Check on Cashbook Bank Balance:

		£
	Opening balance per cashbook – Jan	40492.43
Add	Total bankings per cashbook	44085.75
		84578.18
Less	Total bank payments per cashbook	51644.55
	Bank balance per cashbook c/fwd	**32933.63**

Answer to Exercise 20 (page 137) and Exercise 21 (page 139)

See page 173 (Sales Day Book) and page 174 (Purchase Day Book)

Answer to Exercise 20 (pages 137 and 138)

Sales Day Book

Date	Customer	Inv No	Gross Amount	VAT	Cash Sales Net	Credit Sales Net	Date Paid	Remarks
3/2/199x	Sunspot Ltd	1001	587.50	87.50	500.00			
4/2/199x	Sunspot Ltd	1002	3160.75	470.75		2690.00		
6/2/199x	Venetian Ways	1003	4230.00	630.00		3600.00	19/3/9x	
7/2/199x	Shady Dealings	1004	7637.50	1137.50	6500.00			
8/2/199x	Eclipse Blinds	1005	1504.00	224.00		1280.00		
11/2/199x	Shadowlands	1006	4700.00	700.00	4000.00			
12/2/199x	Sunshield Blds	1007	5722.25	852.25		4870.00		
16/2/199x	Blind Love	1008	3995.00	595.00	3400.00			
23/2/199x	Sunblind Co	1009	2761.25	411.25	2350.00			
24/2/199x	Eclipse Blinds	1020	705.00	105.00		600.00		
Totals			35003.25	5213.25	16750.00	13040.00		

Answer to Exercise 21 (pages 139 and 140)

Purchase Day Book

Date	Supplier	Ref No	Gross Amt	VAT	Net Amt	Date Paid	Stock (net)	Motor (net)	Tel (net)	Stat (net)	Other (net)
1/2/199x	Petrol	150	30.00	4.47	25.53	1/2/9x		25.53			
3/2/199x	Jay's Fabrics	151	11162.50	1662.50	9500.00	3/2/9x	9500.00				
4/2/199x	Die Cast Ltd	152	8812.50	1312.50	7500.00	4/2/9x	7500.00				
6/2/199x	Tool Hire	153	47.00	7.00	40.00	6/2/9x					40.00
6/2/199x	Petrol	154	30.00	4.47	25.53	6/2/9x		25.53			
7/2/199x	The Advertiser	155	881.25	131.25	750.00	7/2/9x					750.00
9/2/199x	Office Supply	156	1410.00	210.00	1200.00	9/2/9x				1200.00	
11/2/199x	Petrol	157	30.00	4.47	25.53	11/2/9x		25.53			
15/2/199x	Office Supply	158	615.00	91.60	523.40	15/2/9x				523.40	
18/2/199x	Petrol	159	30.00	4.47	25.53	18/2/9x		25.53			
21/2/199x	Electric Drill	160	49.35	7.35	42.00	21/2/9x					42.00
24/2/199x	Water Rates	161	890.65	-	890.65	24/2/9x					890.65
26/2/199x	Jay's Fabrics	162	8022.90	1194.90	6828.00	26/2/9x	6828.00				
27/2/199x	Office Supply	163	312.55	46.55	266.00	27/2/9x				266.00	
Totals			32323.70	4681.53	27642.17		23828.00	102.12		1989.40	1722.65

Value Added Tax Return
For the period

HM Customs and Excise

For Official Use

Registration Number | Period

You could be liable to a financial penalty it your completed return and all the VAT payable are not received by the due date.

Due date:

For Official Use

Answer to Exercise 22 (page 141)

Your VAT Office telephone number is

Before you fill in this form please read the notes on the back and the VAT leaflet *"Filling in your VAT return"*. Fill in all boxes clearly in ink, and write 'none' where necessary. Don't put a dash or leave any box blank. If there are no pence write "00" in the pence column. **Do not** enter more than one amount in any box.

		£	p
For official use	**1** VAT due in this period on **sales** and other outputs	5224	27
	2 VAT due in this period on **acquisitions** from other **EC Member States**	None	
	3 Total VAT due **(the sum of boxes 1 and 2)**	5224	27
	4 VAT reclaimed in this period on **purchases** and other inputs (including acquisitions from the EC)	4354	03
	5 Net VAT to be paid to Customs or reclaimed by you **(Difference between boxes 3 and 4)**	870	24
	6 Total value of **sales** and all other outputs excluding any VAT. **Include your box 8 figure**	29853	00
	7 Total value of **purchases** and all other inputs excluding any VAT. **Include your box 9 figure**	24880	00
	8 Total value of all **supplies** of goods and related services, excluding any VAT, to other **EC Member States**	None	00
	9 Total value of all **acquisitions** of goods and related services, excluding any VAT, from other **EC Member States**	None	00

Retail schemes. If you have used any of the schemes in the period covered by this return, enter the relevant letter(s) in this box.

If you are enclosing a payment please tick this box.

DECLARATION: You, or someone on your behalf, must sign below.

I,...declare that the
(Full name of signatory in BLOCK LETTERS)

information given above is true and complete.

Signature...Date.............19......

A false declaration can result in prosecution.

L

VAT 100

Answer to Exercise 23 (page 141)

Sonny Sunblinds — February 19xx

Income

1 Date	2 Detail	3 Total	4 VAT	5 Cash Sales	6 Credit Sales	7 Other Income
Feb 1	Cash Sale	1880 00	280 00	1600 00		
3	Cash Sale	3818 75	568 75	3250 00		
3	Credit Sale	587 50	87 50		500 00	
6	Sale of Machinery	3525 00	525 00			3000 00
7	Cash Sale	7637 50	1137 50	6500 00		
10	Credit Sale	2350 00	350 00		2000 00	
11	Cash Sale	4700 00	700 00	4000 00		
12	Credit Sale	693 25	103 25		590 00	
14	Credit Sale	1175 00	175 00		1000 00	
16	Cash Sale	3995 00	595 00	3400 00		
19	Cash Sale	3818 75	568 75	3250 00		
23	Credit Sale	2761 25	411 25		2350 00	
25	Cash Sale	1468 75	218 75	1250 00		
27	Cash Sale	587 50	87 50	500 00		
28	Cash Sale	5287 50	787 50	4500 00		
	Totals	44285 75	6595 75	28840 00	5850 00	3000 00
	Cash Bal B/Fwd From Jan	55 93				
		44341 68				

Expenditure

8 Date	9 Detail	10 Bankings/Cash Out	11 Bank Payments	12 VAT	13 Materials	14 Travel + Petrol	15 Telephone	16 Light Heat	17 Printing Stat	18 Wages	19 Sundries	20 Banking
Feb 1	Petrol	30 00		4 47		25 53						
2	Banking	1880 00										1880 00
3	Jay's Fabrics		11162 50	1662 50	9500 00							
3	Banking	3818 75										3818 75
3	Wages		5292 20							5292 20		
4	Die Cast Ltd		8812 50	1312 50	7500 00							
6	Tool Hire	47 00		7 00							40 00	
6	Petrol	30 00		4 47		25 53						
7	Advertising		881 25	131 25							750 00	
7	Banking	11550 00										11550 00
9	Stationery		1410 00	210 00					1200 00			
10	Banking	2350 00										2350 00
11	Banking	4700 00										4700 00
11	Petrol	30 00		4 47		25 53						
12	Banking	693 25										693 25
13	New Machinery		14100 00	2100 00							12000 00	
14	Banking	1175 00										1175 00
15	Office Supplies		615 00	91 60					523 40			
18	Petrol	30 00		4 47		25 53						
18	Banking	3995 00										3995 00
19	Banking	3818 75										3818 75
21	Electric Drill	49 35		7 35							42 00	
23	Banking	2761 25										2761 25
24	Water Rates		890 65								890 65	
25	Banking	1468 75										1468 75
26	Jay's Fabrics		8022 90	1194 90	6828 00							
27	Petty Cash		145 00								145 00	
27	Office Stationery		312 55	46 55					266 00			
28	Banking	5875 00										5875 00
	Totals	44302 10	51644 55	6781 53	23828 00	102 12			1989 40	5292 20	13867 65	44085 75
	Cash Bal C/Fwd to March	39 58									Bank Bal B/Fwd From Jan	4049 43
	Bank Bal C/Fwd to March		32933 63									
		44341 68	84578 18									84578 18

VAT and Tax Relief on Bad Debt

If VAT registered traders make supplies of goods or services for which they do not receive payment, they are still liable to pay HMC&E the VAT element of the bad debt. However, there are circumstances in which bad debt relief may be claimed.

Circumstances in which VAT Bad Debt Relief can be Obtained

Traders are able to claim relief from VAT on bad debts providing that all of the following conditions apply.

- The VAT on the bad debt has already been accounted for on your VAT Return. You must have paid the VAT to Customs and Excise.

- The goods or services were supplied in exchange for money.

- The bad debt has been written off in your accounts (details of how to do this are given later).

- The bad debt has been outstanding for at least six months from the date of supply (prior to 1 April 1993, the waiting period was one year) except in the case of the liquidation or insolvency of the supplier.

- Ownership of the goods or services must have passed to the customer. No relief can be claimed on a contract with a 'Romalpa' clause. A Romalpa clause retains title to the goods until payment has been made. However, if goods have been supplied with a Romalpa clause and these goods have not been passed to a third party with title, relief can be claimed provided the retention of title clause is waived.

If your customer has become insolvent, you may need evidence. This is established by some form of official confirmation of inability to pay debts. In the case of a company, this could be a bankruptcy order. You will also need a certificate from the receiver stating that there will be no distribution to creditors.

HM Customs and Excise may require a copy of the tax invoice(s) relating to the supplies on which the bad debt relief is claimed. If a tax invoice has not been issued then some other form of documentation evidencing your supply must be available.

Details of the bad debt should be recorded in a bad debt account to show:

- the name of the customer
- the date and number of the invoice to which the bad debt relates
- the amount you have written off as a bad debt
- the amount of VAT you are claiming as bad debt relief
- the VAT period in which you originally accounted for and paid the VAT
- the VAT period in which you have claimed the refund
- details of any part payments received for the bad debt.

The amount of relief available is normally the VAT charged on the supply or supplies relating to the bad debt. If you establish a separate bad debt account within your records, it will be easy to identify these amounts from the records. If you have received part payment of the debt, you can only claim the VAT amount that is still outstanding.

What Happens if Payment is Received after Claiming Bad Debt Relief?

If, after claiming a refund of VAT on a bad debt, you receive payment then the VAT on the amount subsequently recovered must be repaid to HM Customs and Excise. This is done by simply adding the VAT on the debt recovered to the total amount of the VAT due in the VAT period in which the debt is recovered.

If you are insured against bad debts and the insurance is for the VAT inclusive amount of the bad debt, you may claim this amount even though you have received bad debt relief from Customs and Excise.

Further information concerning VAT relief on bad debts can be obtained from VAT leaflet 700/18/91, available from your local VAT office.

Income Tax Relief for Bad Debts

Bad debt relief for Income Tax purposes is obtained by including the bad debt within the accounts of the business. A provision for bad debts will appear in the profit and loss account as an overhead expense of the business. This will obviously reduce the overall net profit assessable to tax. Income Tax relief may also be available for *doubtful* debts, the Inland Revenue's interpretation of which is discussed below.

The deduction for bad or doubtful debts is made in arriving at the net profit of the year in which the debts become bad or doubtful. Where a deduction is made for doubtful debts, this is generally referred to as a *reserve* for bad debts. Where there is more than one debt included within this reserve, the Inland Revenue ask that the reserve is based on a reasonably accurate valuation of each doubtful debt.

The Inland Revenue will also accept a provision for bad debts after the accounting year ends providing there is evidence that the debt will be bad or doubtful prior to finalisation of the accounts. The Inland Revenue have recently clarified the circumstances where this provision will be allowed. These are:

- A debt existed at the balance sheet date, *and*

- The creditor at that date had no reason to believe that he would not be paid, *but*

- Before the accounts were finalised, he discovered that the financial position of the debtor at the balance sheet date was such that, even at that time, he was unlikely to be paid.

For example, a debt may be owed at the end of the accounting year but the debtor may go into administration or liquidation shortly after the accounting year end but before finalisation of the accounts by the accountant.

There is no statutory period beyond which relief for bad debts can be claimed as there is for VAT purposes. Whether a bad or doubtful debt is claimable is a matter of circumstance and fact. The length of time a debt is outstanding is, on it's own, not sufficient grounds for claiming relief.

Indeed, where an Inspector of Taxes is not satisfied that the deduction claimed for bad or doubtful debts is valid, he will need to establish for each individual debt:

- how the extent of its doubtfulness was evaluated
- when this was done
- by whom
- what information was used in arriving at the evaluation that the debt was bad or doubtful.

Therefore, in order to approve a bad debt claim, the Inspector may require sight of all the evidence available. This may include copies of correspondence with the debtor and third parties concerning the debt, eg solicitors, banks, factoring agencies etc, together with any reports that have been obtained regarding the financial status of the debtor. In addition, the Inspector may wish to see copies of any internal correspondence such as memos and minutes of meetings at which the debt may have been discussed. It is essential that all evidence concerning the ways in which you have sought to recover your debts is preserved, in case the Inspector wants to see them. If you don't have an efficient credit control system, you may find it hard to obtain relief for bad or doubtful debts simply because you cannot supply the evidence that you have tried to collect the debt.

If a bad debt is subsequently recovered, you can enter the amount received as a trading receipt of the accounting period when the money was paid to you.

If you are exposed to bad or doubtful debts, consult your accountant so that a provision can be made in your accounts for the bad debt. Also make available to your accountant any information which will help him to convince the tax man of your valid claim.

Index

Through Kogan Page all readers can enjoy the benefits of Call Sciences' *Personal Assistant*®
- the complete Call Management System

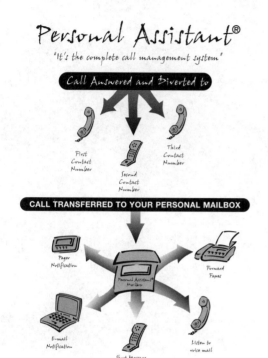

CALL ME – Your clients, friends and family only need ONE NUMBER to contact you rather than separate numbers for mobile, home, office and fax.

FAX ME – You choose where and when your faxes are delivered to any fax machine – you control whether your faxes are forwarded straight away or stored until you collect them.

FIND ME – *Personal Asistant*® searches you at up to 3 locations according to your typical weekly availability schedule – and it even remembers where it last found you.

When you are not available, your calls are automatically routed to voice mail. Whenever a message is received, you are notified by pager, GSM short message or e-mail.

Why have a *Personal Assistant*® number?

- Your own receptionist 24 hours a day
- Your personal number is never engaged
- Greets your callers in a professional manner
- Holds your contact numbers and knows where to find you
- Tells you who is calling before putting them through
- Transfers to another number or voice mail part way through a call
- Knows when you do not normally wish to be disturbed
- Takes voice and fax messages when you are not available
- Faxes delivered to any fax machine
- Charge card option for outgoing calls

All for less than 25p per day

Call Sciences™

QMS ✓
ISO 9002
REGISTERED FIRM

Call 0800 689 9999 today to activate your Personal Assistant®!